ASSERTIVENESS SKILLS
TRAINING

ASSERTIVENESS SKILLS TRAINING

A Sourcebook of Activities

SUE BISHOP

Viva Books Private Limited

New Delhi • Mumbai • Chennai • Kolkata • Bangalore • Hyderabad

First Indian Edition 1996
First Indian Paperback Edition 1999
Reprinted 2002, 2004, 2007

VIVA BOOKS PRIVATE LIMITED

- 4737/23, Ansari Road, Daryaganj, New Delhi 110 002
  E-mail: vivadelhi@vivagroupindia.net, Tel. 42242200
- 215-216 New Apollo Estate, Mogra Lane, Andheri (E), Mumbai 400 069
  E-mail: vivamumbai@vivagroupindia.net, Tel. 56997844, 56997845
- Jamals Fazal Chambers, 26 Greams Road, Chennai 600 006
  E-mail: vivachennai@vivagroupindia.net, Tel. 28290304, 28294241
- B-103, Jindal Towers, 21/1A/3 Darga Road, Kolkata 700 017
  E-mail: vivakolkata@vivagroupindia.net, Tel. 22836381, 22816713
- 7, Sovereign Park Apartments, 56-58, K. R. Road, Basavanagudi, Bangalore 560 004
  E-mail: vivabangalore@vivagroupindia.net, Tel.26607409, 26607410
- 101-102 Mughal Marc Apartments, Narayanguda, Hyderabad 500 029
  E-mail: vivahyderabad@vivagroupindia.net, Tel. 27564481, 27564482

Published by arrangement with

Kogan Page Limited
120 Pentonville Road
London N1 9JN, UK

ISBN 81-7649-017-2

Published by Vinod Vasishtha for Viva Books Private Limited, 4737/23 Ansari Road, Daryaganj, New Delhi 110 002. Printed & bound by Raj Press, R-3 Inderpuri, New Delhi - 110 012.

Contents

Assertiveness training requires participants to take an honest look at themselves; to acknowledge areas where they are non-assertive or aggressive; to recognize the barriers – imposed or self-inflicted – to their behaving assertively. This section has activities which encourage self-appraisal, which help raise confidence and self-esteem, and which examine the total impression we make on others, not only through the words we use and how we deliver them, but also through body language.

While not healthy, or constructive, to dwell for too long on *why* we behave in the way we do, it is helpful to gain some insight into possible causes of our non-assertion and aggression. This section contains activities on conditioning, gender roles and stereotyping. It also has activities on put-downs, and giving and receiving criticism and feedback.

The title of this section is self-explanatory. It includes activities on everyone's basic rights, self-expression, including saying 'yes' and 'no', Broken Record technique, and a sequence of linking activities on what to do when assertive behaviour is not met with the expected response.

This section looks at conflict resolution and how to turn negative situations into positive interactions. It also has one activity which offers 100 different role-play scenarios covering many areas – problem people, money matters, setting limits, harassment and so on.

The changes that result from becoming more assertive can bring their own tension. For some, the training itself can be stressful; the mention of 'role-plays' can reduce some to a jelly-like state! Taking an assertive stance for the first time can cause initial anxiety; tackling long-established interpersonal conflicts can cause stress. This section offers six different relaxation techniques which can be practised during the course, and used prior to difficult encounters.

This section offers three activities to round off a training course with post course follow-up suggestions.

Acknowledgements

My thanks, as always, to Mags for her patience, encouragement and support; also to June Barnett for her help and guidance.

Introduction

If you are a busy trainer, eager to check out and put into practice the activities of this book, you won't want to spend too long reading a lengthy introduction – so I'll keep it short.

This book is intended for use by any professional trainer or manager who is already well versed in basic assertiveness skills and familiar with the principles of assertiveness training. It does not, therefore, offer detailed information on theory, terminology, or techniques. Of course, formal trainer input on these elements is necessary in any session or course of training in assertiveness, and should be followed by practical application of techniques, and skills practice.

This book provides a comprehensive selection of activities that will test participants' understanding of assertiveness. Activities relate to both personal and work situations, so application can be varied. Almost all are stand-alone activities which can be used as a dip-in resource to supplement your training programmes. Some activities are better run in a sequence, and guidance is given on how to link them to create more comprehensive training sessions. Together, the activities include most of the elements you need to run a complete course on assertiveness.

The book has been written with the busy trainer in mind, and every help has been given to reduce preparation time to an absolute minimum. The activities have step-by-step instructions, with detailed processing guidance including relevant questions you might wish to put to your group.

I firmly believe that any training event – whether it is a management game, a discussion, viewing a video or whatever – should contain five elements:

- *An introduction.* This is trainer input in some form to put people's minds at rest as to what is involved, to explain what is expected of them, to give relevant background information, suggest timings and so on.
- *The event itself.* Watching a training film; completing a questionnaire; skills practice etc.
- *Unpacking the experience of the event.* People need time and space to talk about the video, or how they felt about an exercise, or the feelings evoked by a group discussion.
- *Drawing out the learning points.* For example, identifying the message beneath the surface story line of a training film, or establishing the significance of a management game, or analysing why one approach to a problem worked, while another was less successful. It involves summing up the event, stressing again its purpose and how the objectives have been met through the activity. This is probably the most important part of running an event, yet some trainers skimp on this processing element, leaving participants thinking 'What was that all about then?'
- *Applying the learning.* The benefits of training are only truly effective when learning gained in the course room is put into practice in real life. It is the trainer's responsibility to help participants translate theoretical learning into practical use in their daily lives.

Finally, a few personal observations on assertiveness training. All of this is, I hope, preaching to the converted, but nevertheless needs stressing.

Because assertiveness training requires a greater awareness of self and your impact on others, it follows that you – as trainer – need to be a role model for your participants.

Assertiveness training can be of immense benefit to everyone, not just as a skill in itself, but as a means of modifying behaviour, of gaining confidence, of enhancing self-esteem and of cultivating honest, powerful and effective communication.

Assertiveness training increases people's range of choices. It can involve breaking away from familiar, stereotypical patterns of behaviour, looking for alternative, more effective ways of communicating.

Course participants need to understand that assertive interactions involve at least two people, and that for every right *one* person has, the other person has exactly similar rights.

Assertiveness means taking responsibility for your own life, feelings and actions. This will involve change – in self-perception, and in relationships with others. Participants should be aware both of the advantages and risks involved. Effective training will, of course, ensure that the former outweighs the latter!

CHAPTER 1

ICE-BREAKERS AND OPENERS

GETTING TO KNOW YOU

An ice-breaker not only starts individuals communicating with other participants, but sets the tone for some of the training sessions to come.

Objectives By the end of this activity participants will:

- have spoken with many of their course colleagues;
- have experienced low risk self-disclosure;
- have given initial thought to some issues relevant to assertiveness.

Resources Copy of **Trainer's notes**.

Time 30 minutes.

Method
Step 1: Explain the activity This is an activity intended to help people get to know each other – or to know each other better if already colleagues. Participants will stand in two lines, A and B, facing each other. The trainer will call out a question, or suggest a topic which facing pairs will discuss for a few minutes. Then the person on the left-hand end of line A will move to the left-hand end of line B; the person on the right-hand end of line B will move to the right-hand

end of line A thus effectively rotating the lines in a clockwise direction so that new facing pairings are formed. (Have faith – it does work. If nothing else, the confusion caused by these instructions should get the group relaxed and laughing!)

The exercise continues with discussion, rotation, different pairing/ topic for discussion until everyone has had the chance to speak with every other course member, or the trainer runs out of topics!

Step 2: Divide the group into two lines, A and B, facing each other If there is an odd number of participants, the activity will have to be 'stage-managed' so that with each rotation a different triad, rather than pairing, is formed.

Step 3: Suggest facing participants introduce themselves if not already known to each other. Ask the first question or give the first topic for discussion (See **Trainer's notes** for suggestions.)

Step 4: After a few minutes, or when participants seem to have exhausted the topic, begin the rotation process described above The activity continues in this way, with a different question given with each rotation.

Step 5: End the exercise Use your discretion regarding how long to continue the activity.

Step 6: Reconvene the main group for a general discussion of some of the issues raised Ask for comments on the activity itself, then on the topics discussed. Individuals may offer their own views, but if self-disclosure was involved, it should be stressed that confidences should not be broken.

Step 7: Sum up by setting some of the topics in context of the assertiveness training programme to follow. Close the activity by referring to the objectives

TRAINER'S NOTES

Getting to know you

Eavesdropping on some of the discussions can give valuable insight into the confidence and self-esteem of individuals within the group. It goes without saying that no comment should be made to the group about any of these perceptions.

Below are some suggestions of questions you might use or topics you might cover which have a bearing on the content of assertiveness training programmes. There are 15 questions which allows for a course of 30 people. Please use these at your own discretion, amending as you think fit, or adding ones of your own.

- What is your favourite leisure activity?
- Why did you choose to wear today the clothes you are wearing now?
- How do you relax?
- If you weren't you, who would you like to be?
- Generally speaking, do women or men get a better deal out of life?
- What, if anything, makes you feel emotional?
- What sort of childhood did you have?
- Who, living or dead, do you most admire, and why?
- What is your greatest achievement?
- What are the positive qualities you bring to your work?
- What things in life give you pleasure?
- What do you like most about yourself?
- What can you do better than most people?
- What are you most proud of in your life?
- If you had unlimited resources, what would you buy which would give you most pleasure?

SMALL TALK

An ice-breaker which gives participants a chance to practise their skills in making small talk. Often, people attend assertiveness training courses to overcome shyness and feelings of low self-esteem. They sometimes find it difficult to communicate on a superficial level, and so avoid social gatherings. This activity is especially useful if run with participants previously unknown to each other.

Objectives By the end of this activity participants will:

- have 'broken the ice' by speaking with several other course members.

Resources Copy of **Trainer's notes**.

Time 15 minutes.

Method

Step 1: Introduce and explain the activity In any course about communication or assertiveness, it is important to articulate your opinions, feelings and so on. This will be required of everyone during the course, yet often the thought of uttering those first few words in public can be quite daunting.

There may well also be some people on the course who find it difficult to communicate, especially in groups, and especially with people not well known to them. This activity 'breaks the ice' gently by giving everyone the opportunity to talk with several course colleagues.

Working in pairs, you will be given a subject on which to chat –

make small talk – for about a minute. Then you will be asked to move on to a different partner, be given a new topic to chat about, and so on until you've had the chance to chat with several people – and the trainer's ideas for topics run out!

Step 2: Divide the group into pairs Instruct participants to find partners and to spread around the outside of the room. It doesn't matter who their present partner is – whether or not they are known to each other – because after a minute or so they will be moved on to form another, different pairing. Ask participants to decide which is to be A or B.

Step 3: Circulate around the group giving each pair a topic on which to make small talk (See **Trainer's notes**.) Instruct the As to initiate the conversation, ie make the opening remarks.

Step 4: After a minute or so, instruct Bs to move to the As to the right of them, thus forming different pairings Repeat Step 3 above, but this time the Bs should initiate the small talk.

Step 5: After another minute or so, instruct participants to change partners again Repeat Steps 3 and 4 another couple of times.

Step 6: Reconvene the main group Ask for reactions to the activity. *Questions you might use:*

- Do any of you usually find it difficult to make small talk? Why? (Typical responses: 'I'm not witty enough'; 'I'm boring'; 'I can't keep a conversation "light"'; 'I'm too self-conscious'; 'I can't think of anything to say.')
- How can these negative feelings be overcome?
- How might concentrating on the other person's needs and feelings be helpful?
- In what ways would having several topics 'up your sleeve' be useful? (Typical responses: 'To have an opening, plus a couple of other topics if conversation dries'; To have topics appropriate to situations/individuals'; 'To give me more confidence'.)
- Why is it important for you to be able to initiate small talk? (Typical responses: 'To show the other person that I am interested in them'; 'So that I can ask the questions, then leave the other person to do the talking'; 'So that people will like me – and invite me again!')
- When might it be important for you to be able to initiate small

talk? (Typical responses: At work – left alone with a client. Socially – at parties; generally meeting people for the first time.)

- What have you learned from the activity?

Step 7: Thank the group for participating. Close the activity by referring to the objectives

TRAINER'S NOTES

Small talk

Some suggested topics for small talk:

- How did you get to the course?
- What's your preferred method of travel?
- What do you hope to get out of the course?
- What type of house do you live in?
- Do you enjoy theatre? Ballet? Opera? etc?
- Have you had a holiday this year?
- What sort of work do you do?
- Have you got any children? Grandchildren? Pets?
- Do you enjoy doing exercises like this?

No doubt, you will be able to think of others relevant to your group. These are just some ideas to get you started. The point of the activity is to get people talking to each other (break the ice) and develop their ability to confidently engage in spontaneous conversation with others.

THE STORY OF . . .

This is a well tried ice-breaker activity which is especially useful on assertiveness programmes because it gives the trainer an immediate 'snapshot' of the characters of participants represented – those who are happy with self-disclosure; those who are self-effacing; those whose body language betrays them, and so on. Because participants are asked to talk about an object, rather than themselves, it is a less stressful ice-breaker than some.

Objectives By the end of this activity participants will:

- have spoken for some time in front of the group;
- have had the opportunity to learn something about other group members.

Resources None.

Time Allow 3 or 4 minutes per participant.

Method

Step 1: Explain the activity Participants will be asked to tell the rest of the group about any item they choose which they are wearing or carrying with them. That's all there is to it – just talk for about a minute about a personal possession they have with them.

Step 2: Allow participants a couple of minutes to decide which item they are going to tell the group about, and to gather their thoughts together

Step 3: Decide who is going to be first to tell 'The story of . . .' Ask for volunteers or choose any means of picking one! Do not 'go round the circle' in a systematic way as this can cause anxiety in nervous participants, and makes it virtually impossible for those next in line to concentrate and listen well.

Step 4: Run the activity until everyone has described a personal possession You can include yourself in the activity, of course.

Step 5: Thank participants for their contributions, sum up, and close the activity by referring to the objectives Acknowledge that for everyone attending a new course, one of the most difficult things to do is to make that first contribution. Now everyone has spoken in public, so a major hurdle has been overcome.

THE CONTRACT

Run this activity at the beginning of the course. It allows participants to express their needs or apprehensions, and sets the ground rules for the duration of the training. It could usefully be followed by the activity **First impressions.**

Objectives By the end of this activity participants will:

- have identified and agreed standards which will be adhered to by all participants, and the trainer, for the duration of the course;
- have had an initial opportunity to practice assertion skills – expressing needs, opinions, doubts and so on in a positive and constructive way.

Resources Flipchart paper and marker, and means of fixing flipchart sheets to the wall.

Time 15–30 minutes.

Method
Step 1: Explain the purpose of, and procedure for, the activity It is important for all participants attending any training event to feel comfortable with the environment, with each other, with the content of the programme, and with the trainer, if maximum learning is to take place. This is especially important in assertiveness training where individuals' attitudes, patterns of behaviour, and methods of self expression are analysed. This activity allows the trainer and participants to work out some ground rules which can be agreed by all. These will be recorded on flipchart paper, and attached to a wall

where they can be seen and referred to if necessary during the course. The completed sheet will serve as a contract between the trainer and the participants throughout the course.

Step 2: Begin the activity by suggesting the sorts of areas participants may wish to consider These can be general issues such as time-keeping; eg the trainer will ensure each session finishes promptly provided everyone returns from refreshment breaks at the agreed time; or arrangements for smoking; or whether participants have to wait for coffee or meal breaks to go to the loo!

They could also be more course-specific; eg if there is to be a session requiring a degree of self-disclosure, participants should only reveal what they feel comfortable about. No pressure will be exerted to 'reveal all!'

Other issues which participants may wish to include in the contract: eg some participants are reluctant to have their poor spelling exposed by participating in flipchart-type activities, so a 'spelling doesn't matter' entry could be included in the contract for the course.

You may feel it necessary to include terminology 'rules' such as the use of the word 'black' to describe, generically, people of Asian, African or Afro-Caribbean origin; or the word 'partner' to describe, generically, the person with whom participants share their lives.

The **Trainer's notes** give further guidance on issues for possible inclusion in the contract.

Step 3: Use good 'chairing' skills to ensure that everyone has the opportunity to express their views on each issue, and/or to put forward other suggestions for consideration by the group. As each point is agreed, find a suitable phrase to record the group decision on the flipchart contract It may be necessary to use your authority as 'leader' to help the group reach a decision, or to explain why it is necessary to include some items. For example, you may feel it essential that everyone listen when another is speaking; or to record that everyone's contribution should be respected; or that a company's rules on equal opportunities are enforced on the course, or comments and criticism should be positive and constructive at all times, and so on.

Step 4: When ideas have been exhausted, and everything agreed has been listed, ask finally if everyone is happy with the contract which will serve as ground rules for the course. If everyone is in agreement,

pin the list to a wall where it can be easily seen and referred to if necessary Items should not be removed from the list once it is agreed unless by group decision. It may be necessary to add rules at a later date, but the above procedure should be adopted to ensure whole group agreement.

TRAINER'S NOTES

The contract

These are some of the contract agreements, and arguments for their inclusion, which frequently occur on assertiveness training courses. Others are listed and discussed briefly in the '***Method***' of this activity, and of course each training programme will produce its own points for inclusion. This is intended as a guide only.

Confidentiality Participants are often reluctant to express true feelings on courses for fear of ridicule, or that someone will tell others, outside the course room, of confidences expressed during training sessions. You should include yourself in this clause. You should assure participants that you won't be telling tales to bosses, or disclosing information revealed on the course. In other words, everyone must agree to be supportive, and to agree that confidences will not go beyond the training rooms.

Organizational policies remain in force The above condition does not exempt participants from adhering to organizational rules, however. If, for example, you are running an in-company course where there exists an equal opportunities policy, participants could not express overtly racist views under cover of the 'Confidentiality' clause. The difference should be pointed out between offensive racist remarks and meaningful discussion of race issues. This clause could, of course, refer to any company rules which individuals *might* feel could be waived under the confidentiality clause.

Respect for others While not agreeing with everyone's opinions, views should be respected. The word 'respect' obviously covers a wide area. For example, sometimes participants do not understand that something which is easy for them can be very difficult for another person, and remarks like 'Well, you shouldn't let her get away with it; just tell her that...' may be made. Individuals' *feelings* in a given situation are legitimate, and should be respected.

Listen to each other It is easy – and common – on training courses, for ideas presented by the central speaker, whether it be trainer or participant, to spark off splinter-group discussions. Groups of two or three can often be seen whispering, and not concentrating on the speaker. Bearing the above clause in mind, this shows little respect for the individual who is trying to address the whole group, or for colleagues who may be distracted by these asides. The skill of listening is one which is generally practised on assertiveness training courses.

Honesty When asked what they would like included in the contract, participants often say 'honesty'. This will need some discussion. Honesty will be needed, for example, when giving constructive feedback during group work. Honest, clear and direct communication is certainly an important aspect of assertive behaviour, but agreeing to be honest at all times could prove an embarrassment and disincentive to some participants. In order to create and maintain a secure and supportive environment, the following clause should also be added to the contract.

Share only what you want to share Participants may be concerned about self-disclosure elements in assertiveness courses and may not want to reveal aspects of their lives, feelings, emotions, preferring to keep parts of their lives private. This clause protects such wishes.

Timekeeping Often, especially when a training programme continues over a few days or weeks, timekeeping becomes lax – not just on the part of the participants who may arrive late, or linger over coffee or meal breaks, but with the trainer. Returning to the 'respect' clause, it is unfair to participants who always arrive punctually for sessions to have to wait for the more tardy. Similarly, it is not showing respect for canteen staff, for example, if the trainer allows sessions to run into refreshment breaks. Many participants will have family commitments, or difficult travel arrangements. They will need to leave the day's session promptly. Mutual respect needs to be shown with regard to timekeeping.

Smoking Unless the training venue has a firm policy on smoking, a consensus will need to be reached on when and where smoking will be acceptable. Generally, participants will agree to smoke only at official refreshment breaks in areas designated for smoking.

FIRST IMPRESSIONS

This is an optional follow-up activity to **The contract**. It is a variation on the mutual introduction theme – a 'getting to know you' exercise – which addresses issues raised by the previous activity, thus giving a focus for paired discussion.

Objectives By the end of this activity participants will:

- have met, and spoken with at least one other course member;
- have had the opportunity to discuss more fully the issues raised by the contract;
- have a greater appreciation of the complexity of self-expression in varying situations
- have made one short presentation to the whole group.

Resources None.

Time 30 minutes to one hour, depending on the total number of participants.

Method
Step 1: Explain the procedure and timings of the activity The group will be divided into pairs – one triad if there is an odd number. After initial introductions, and 'getting to know you' formalities, pairs will look at the various issues raised by the contract and chat around these issues more fully. For example, if one of the points recorded is 'listen to each other', share times when either you have not listened carefully to another person, or when you have not been listened to. Explore your reactions to both situations, and the effect your inattention may have had on another person.

If one of the points on the contract referred to smoking, discuss your own views on this issue; whether or not you were fully happy with the group decision; times when you would have liked to communicate your views, eg asked someone not to smoke in a restaurant, or, conversely, express your rights to smoke when it was obviously resented. It may be, of course, that individuals *did* express their views. How was this done, and what was the outcome?

Take each of the issues raised and discuss in the sort of depth illustrated by the above examples.

Pairs will be allowed 15 minutes for this part of the activity.

At the end of 15 minutes, pairs will be asked to introduce their partner, and to share their observations with the group.

Step 2: Divide the group into pairs (one triad if necessary) Use any means to do this. If everyone knows each other, the pairings can be arbitrary. If just a few people are acquainted, try to arrange pairings so that each person is talking to someone not previously well known to them.

Step 3: Circulate round the pairs, establishing whether they are keeping 'on target' Advise on procedure, and areas for debate, but do not get involved in discussions at this stage.

Step 4: After 15 minutes establish whether pairs are ready to return to the main group for plenary discussion If necessary, and you think it would be useful, you could negotiate more time. An extra 5 minutes should be sufficient, however.

Step 5: Return to the main group. Ask pairs, in turn, to say a few words of introduction about their partner; then to share with the group any observations about the issues on the contract If, say, there are 8 items on the contract and 8 or fewer pairings, it might be preferable for each pair to 'lead' on one item, and their observations then thrown open for general discussion by the group. Whichever method is chosen, it is important that every member of the group be given the opportunity to (*a*) introduce their partner, and (*b*) report on some aspect of their discussion.

Step 6: When each item has been covered, ask some general questions about the two activities – 'The contract' and 'First impressions' – drawing out learning points, and again encouraging participation from everyone. Good assertive techniques should be fostered, ie listening skills, constructive feedback, and so on.

Questions you might use:

- Did you find it easier contributing to the main group input in **The contract**, or discussing the issues with just one (or two) other(s)? Why?
- Were you more, or less concerned about airing your views to just one person? Why? Did you phrase your communication differently when speaking to a group of people? In what way? Were you comfortable with an element of self-disclosure in each instance? Why, or why not?
- Generally, how did people's anxieties, or frustrations, or annoyances manifest themselves to others – in words? in tone of voice? in body language? Can you give examples?
- In what way do you feel that setting a contract is a productive way of opening a course on assertiveness? Are there any disadvantages?

Step 7: Close the activity, referring to the objectives of both 'The contract' and 'First impressions' By now, if participants have had any anxieties about attending a course on assertiveness, they should have had the opportunity to communicate their views and to negotiate terms of reference with the group. By debating issues in this way, participants have had an initial opportunity to practise assertion skills – talking about needs, expressing opinions, listening to, and accommodating others' views, and so on. So without having any formal input on assertive practice, participants have already been rehearsing some of the skills of assertion – skills which will be looked at in more depth later in the course.

Hopefully, by now everyone feels more comfortable within the group, and has spoken in depth with at least one other person. Also, the ice has been broken in terms of contributing to sessions on the course. Having to speak in front of a group for the first time can cause anxiety for some people. It is a milestone which everyone has now survived!

WHY ARE WE HERE?

A simple, group work activity, to be run at the beginning of a course of assertiveness training, to establish what participants hope to gain from the training.

Objectives By the end of this activity participants will:

- have established the reasons for attending this course of training;
- have expressed what they hope to gain from the training;
- have discussed aspects which might help or hinder the training.

Resources Notepaper, pens/pencils, flipchart and marker.

Time 1 hour.

Method
Step 1: Explain the procedure and timings for the activity In groups participants will be asked to discuss and list four things:

(1) Their reasons for attending.
(2) Things which will help them to achieve this learning.
(3) Things which will hinder the learning.
(4) Any worries or concerns about assertiveness training.

It may be useful to summarise these four points on the flipchart.

Participants will have 20–30 minutes to discuss these four points. The group will then reconvene and a composite, flipchart list drawn up. This list can be pinned to a wall for future reference. (*Optional*) – the list can be typed up and issued later as a Handout.

Step 2: Divide participants into groups of no more than five people

More than this number and it is unlikely that the most reticent will contribute to the discussion.

Step 3: Issue notepaper and pens/pencils. Set the groups to work Give a time check after 20 minutes to see how groups are progressing. Negotiate a finishing time.

Step 4: Reconvene the main group. Draw up a composite list on the flipchart from the groups' work Take one point from each group in turn so that everyone has the chance to fully contribute. Check whether the view expressed is the view of the whole group or just of one or two individuals. Discuss any points arising from included items.

Step 5: Add any comments of your own It may be that there are omissions which you feel need discussion. For example, no-one may have included 'To become less aggressive' as a reason for attending. This may be because individuals don't recognize aggressive behaviour in themselves – don't see sarcasm or patronizing behaviour as aggressive – or that they see aggression as something to be admired – as macho, or beating men at their own game, or the only way to survive in business. (See **Trainer's notes**.)

Step 6: Sum up and close the activity by referring to the objectives Thank the group for contributing in such an honest way. Reassure about any fears which were expressed. Undertake to include whatever is realistic and feasible to meet individuals' needs.

TRAINER'S NOTES

Why are we here?

The following lists are a compilation from courses run by the author. As you will see from the list, some of these will need discussion (see the sixth bullet point, for example).

Reasons for coming

- to be able to handle conflict
- to be more assertive with my boss
- to gain self-confidence
- to become less aggressive
- to be able to express myself better
- to be able to win more arguments when I know I'm right
- to be able to deal with work situations better
- to communicate honestly with my partner
- to be able to cope with a difficult situation without getting emotional.
- to stop feeling guilty for standing up for myself
- to improve my interpersonal communication
- to be able to realize my full potential
- to be able to turn confrontation into adult to adult discussion
- so that I can stop people pushing me around
- to control my temper; to stop over-reacting
- to be able to take a few more risks in my life
- to improve my quality of life

What will help the learning to take place

- support from the group
- confidentiality
- openness
- 'safe' environment
- trust
- able to give and take constructive criticism
- sense of humour – laughing *with* each other
- sharing personal experiences
- self-disclosure
- co-operating
- forgiving

What will hinder learning taking place

- not participating
- shyness
- embarrassment
- being afraid to make mistakes
- conflict
- mistrust
- reluctance to share
- cliques or 'in-groups'
- negative criticism
- humour at the expense of others
- feeling isolated
- being afraid to express a contentious opinion
- being obstructive

Worries or concerns about assertiveness training

- being made to look silly
- not being able to participate fully (shyness)
- role plays
- that relationships with family and friends might change
- that I won't be able to cope
- self-disclosure
- confidentiality.

CHAPTER 2

GETTING STARTED

COLD SOUP

This activity tests participants' understanding of the terminology used in assertiveness training. It should be run *after* formal input on the meaning and usage of the terms 'assertive', 'passive', 'aggressive' and 'manipulative'.

Objectives By the end of this activity participants will:

- each have had the opportunity to assign a statement to one of the four terms listed above;
- have considered how choice of vocabulary, tone of voice and differing situations can change interpretation of meaning;
- better understand the concepts of assertive, passive, aggressive and manipulative behaviour.

Resources Approximately 4 metres of string or cord, 16 blank post-cards, copy of **Trainer's notes**, flipchart and coloured markers.

Time 1 hour.

Method

Step 1: Arrange seating in a horseshoe with space in the 'jaws' for the flipchart. Place the string on the floor in a broad-based triangle shape with cards along base and at apex *(see* **Trainer's notes.***)*

Step 2: Introduce the activity, explaining procedure This activity will help participants to consolidate their understanding of the terminology which will be used during training sessions.

The base of the triangle represents a continuum from passive to aggressive behaviour with assertiveness being the balance between the two. The lines from passive to manipulative at the point of the triangle, and from aggressive to manipulative are also continua.

Imagine this scene. You have been asked to discuss a business proposition with an important client over lunch and have taken her or him to an expensive restaurant. You have both chosen soup as a starter. When it arrives it is cold. As you are the host, you feel you should do something about the situation.

Each participant will receive a card with a possible response written on it. Some responses will appear rational; others will obviously be extreme; most will be debatable in the context of assertive behaviour.

In turn participants will be asked to place their cards on the continua, and to explain their decision for that placing. The group can question and discuss the choice, and the card can be moved if the 'owner' so desires.

This continues until every card is placed somewhere on the triangle.

Step 3: Issue cards (previously completed as shown in the Trainer's notes) If there are fewer than 12 course members, either issue more than one card to some participants, or be selective in the cards offered. Some responses share similar learning points.

Step 4: Begin the activity Either ask participants, in turn, to reproduce what is written on their card on the flipchart before placing the card on the triangle, or to read it out for you to reproduce on flipchart paper. It is important that the whole group *see* the words, because nuances could affect the choice of where the card is eventually placed on the continua.

Step 5: Question choices for placings if appropriate, always encouraging other group members to contribute to the discussion. *Points to consider:*

Card 1 – There are recipes where the soup is *meant* to be cold. If it is meant as a sarcastic response, sarcasm is always aggressive, so the placing should reflect that. If it is said as a joke, would this make any

difference? Could this response be seen as manipulative in any way, ie could it be intended as an opener to further discussion?
Card 2 – What is the likely response of the waiter if food is just left? If he merely clears the plates, what is achieved? If the waiter asks if there was anything wrong, what sort of behaviour prompted this?
Card 3 – What are the legal implications of walking out without paying? What has this gesture achieved? Does it have manipulative undertones?
Card 4 – What effect is this likely to have on the client? the other diners? the waiter? What is this comment and the way it was delivered likely to achieve? Is it fair to put off potential customers without first giving the establishment the chance to remedy things?
Card 5 – In what way could this be seen as aggressive? Should the waiter be first given a chance to put things right? How is the waiter likely to respond? In what way is it therefore manipulative behaviour? If the word 'please' had been used, would it have been less aggressive?
Card 6 – Are there any circumstances when this response would not be an assertive one? It is a perfectly reasonable request, especially if you haven't the time for a replacement to be brought.
Card 7 – What effect would these comments have on the waiter, and on the client? What was achieved?
Card 8 – Can this be seen as anything other than sarcastic?
Card 9 – Does this ring any bells?! Would anyone like to share an experience they have had of this?
Card 10 – Can anyone find fault with this? Assuming that the tone of voice is appropriate, would you agree that this is an assertive response?
Card 11 – What message are you sending to the client?
Card 12 – What are these comments likely to achieve? Are there any occasions when manipulative behaviour can be seen as passive?

Step 6: Proceed until all the cards have been placed. Briefly process the activity.

Questions you might use:

- Having looked at various ways of responding to a difficult predicament, what would you now do if faced with a similar situation?

- Is it more fair and assertive to give the person in the front line – in this case the waiter – a chance to put things right?
- Is there a case for giving feedback to the manager or owner of the establishment? How would you do this?
- Can you see parallels in your own social or working life where this kind of assertive behaviour might be practised?

Step 7: Close the activity by referring to the learning objectives
Participants should now have a clearer idea of what is meant by each of the four behaviour patterns, but recognize that there are many variations to each theme. Different situations, relationships, nuances and so on can affect the way our communication is received.

TRAINER'S NOTES

Cold soup

Take four of the postcards and write the words PASSIVE, ASSERTIVE, AGGRESSIVE AND MANIPULATIVE on them. Place them on the broad-based triangle, created with string or cord, as shown below.

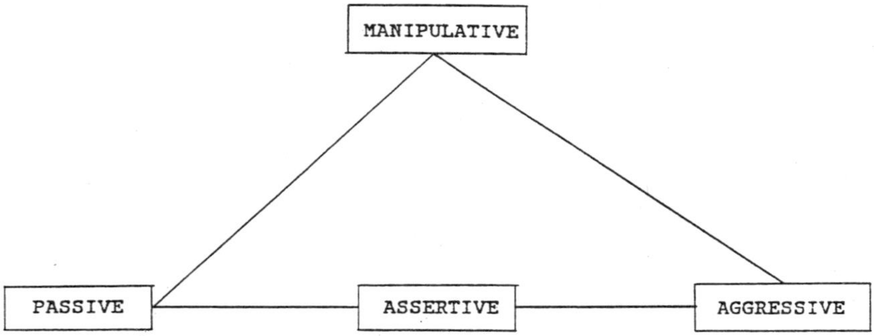

On the other cards, write the following responses:

(1) Say to the waiter 'Is this soup supposed to be cold?'
(2) Leave the soup.
(3) Walk out.
(4) Complain loudly, and in the hearing of the waiter and several other diners, 'It's the last time I shall bring anyone here.'
(5) Tell the waiter 'I'd like to see the manager.'
(6) Tell the waiter that you would like the price of the soup deducted from the bill.
(7) Say to the waiter 'This soup is disgusting. Take it away and bring us some decently prepared food at once.'

(8) Ask the waiter 'Is there something wrong with your electricity supply?'
(9) Eat the soup anyway.
(10) Say to the waiter 'This soup is cold. Would you replace it please?'
(11) Ask the client if she or he wants to complain about the soup.
(12) When the waiter comes to collect the dishes say 'I'm sorry but I'm afraid we couldn't finish the soup. The flavour was quite nice but it was not very warm – quite cold in fact.'

What if?

An activity to be run early in a course, this offers several sample situations and asks participants what they would do if.... Obviously, not every difficult situation can be represented, but through discussion, participants should have a better idea of the kinds of areas where they are presently non-assertive, and where practice and help is needed. It could usefully be followed by **Ladder of success**.

Objectives By the end of this activity participants will:

- have discussed, with at least one other person, areas where assertion skills need to be practised;
- be better equipped to undertake follow-up activities such as **Ladder of success** and **Be prepared**.

Resources One copy of the Exercise Sheet for each participant.

Time 45 minutes to one hour.

Method

Step 1: Introduce the activity Assertiveness training demands honest self-awareness. You must really *know* yourself: recognize and acknowledge your good points, but accept every aspect of your nature, 'warts and all'.

In the early stages of training, it is often difficult to recognize areas of your life where you are not as assertive as you might be, or where you are likely to over-react. This activity is designed to aid discussion about such areas.

Step 2: Explain the procedure and timings Participants will each be given an Exercise Sheet on which is listed 50 'what do you do if...' type questions. Time will be allowed to read through the exercise (5 minutes). Working in pairs (or small groups – trainer's choice) participants will then use these questions to aid discussion of their own experiences – where they have been assertive or unassertive. A time check will be given after 30 minutes, and times renegotiated if necessary.

Step 3: Issue the Exercise Sheet. Divide the group into pairs/small groups Explain that some people will not have experience of some of the sample situations on the Exercise Sheet, but will be able to recall and recount *similar* situations in their own lives. The exercise is not to be taken too literally, but used as an aid to discussion within pairs/groups. Stress that if an individual is unhappy with one of the questions, she or he need not discuss it. Participants need only share what they want to share (see **The Contract**).

Step 4: Begin the exercise Circulate among pairs/groups, offering guidance if necessary.

Step 5: Check progress after 30 minutes. Renegotiate times if necessary It is not essential that everyone discusses every statement – individuals can continue the self-awareness process in their own time – but it is important that several situations from each area are discussed.

Step 6: Lead a short plenary session to sum up Ask participants for general comments and observations. Sum up by referring to the objectives, explaining that the aim of the exercise was to allow individuals to consider different aspects of their lives in order to recognize problem areas which can be worked on during the training to follow. Encourage participants to keep the Exercise Sheet, and think about, in their own time, any issues not discussed in pairs/groups.

Step 7: Close the activity

EXERCISE

What if?

Work

What do you do if...

(1) your boss introduces a new system which you can see to be flawed?

(2) your boss finds an error in your work, and chastises you in front of your colleagues?

(3) your boss criticizes you unjustly (in private)?

(4) a member of your team is constantly late for duty?

(5) one of the senior management team makes a pass at you at the staff Christmas party?

(6) during office hours, two of your staff spend an excessive amount of time chatting about their private lives?

(7) your boss expects you to shoulder more responsibility than you feel you are paid for, or your status reflects.

(8) you know your standard of work to be high – possibly better than most in your section – but your employer is ultra-critical of you?

(9) your boss by-passes you and admonishes one of your staff for shoddy work?

(10) you feel that your boss is possessive of information which you need to run your section effectively?

(11) you take a group of clients out to lunch, but the waiter ignores you, addressing a member of your group as if he were the organizer of the party.

(12) you are asked to take on additional work, although you are working to full capacity now?

(13) a customer/client is rude and abusive to you on the telephone?
(14) a customer/client is rude and abusive to one of your staff?
(15) a customer/client makes a racist/sexist remark which you find offensive?

Home

What do you do if...

(16) your partner persists in a habit which annoys you.
(17) your partner refuses to discuss problems and just goes silent and moody?
(18) your partner cannot discuss problems without getting angry, defensive or aggressive?
(19) you always go on holiday with your partner/family, but this year would like to go away on your own or with a friend?
(20) your partner wants a sea, sun and sand holiday but you would prefer a touring holiday to places of cultural interest?
(21) your partner accepts an invitation on your behalf (and you would prefer not to accept)?
(22) you want to begin a hobby which involves a lot of expense?
(23) you want to begin a hobby which involves a lot of time away from home?
(24) after asking for your partner's opinion, you don't agree with her/his advice?
(25) your children do not do enough to help in the house?
(26) you feel you need more privacy/space in your relationship?
(27) your partner feels you need more privacy/space in your relationship?
(28) one of your parents criticizes you about the way you are handling your relationship/bringing up your children?
(29) your partner wants to invite friends to stay, but you have nothing in common with them – don't much like them in fact?
(30) your partner is feeling amorous, but you are not in the mood?

General

What do you do if...

(31) you buy a sweater from a market trader. After one wash, the colours run and it shrinks to a third of its original size?
(32) a colleague persists in asking questions about your private life which you would prefer not to talk about?

(33) you are about to begin a meal in a restaurant. A man at the next table, who has just ordered his coffee, lights up a cigar?

(34) you meet 'the village bore' in the local supermarket, and he wants to tell you about his latest hobby – taxidermy?

(35) you look at your Christmas present list and decide that you don't really like half the people on it! Gift buying has become an expensive ritual?

(36) you are sunbathing on a beach, and the quiet is shattered by a group of young people with a portable CD player?

(37) someone pushes in front of you in a queue?

(38) you are overcharged in a restaurant?

(39) a doctor tells you that you have chronic 'knotakluvirus' and you will need to take 4 capsules of 'Nastistuf' daily?

(40) you go to a solicitor for advice on making a will, and after small talk (which you do understand) she/he launches into legal jargon (which you don't!)?

(41) a friend makes what you consider to be an unreasonable request?

(42) in a shop, a salesperson goes to a lot of trouble to try and find something which will suit you – but nothing does?

(43) someone telephones just as you are sitting down to a meal?

(44) you feel angry/hurt at the way a friend has treated you?

(45) someone is being cruel and insulting about a person you like and admire?

(46) you are chatting with a group of friends, and one person makes a remark about/to you which you feel to be a put-down?

(47) a friend persistently uses you as a shoulder to cry on?

(48) a friend asks to borrow some money?

(49) you need to ask for the repayment of a loan?

(50) a policeman is unnecessarily patronizing and officious to you?

LADDER OF SUCCESS

This activity asks participants to look at areas of their lives where they would like to be more assertive, and to list and prioritize the ten of most importance to them. The activity should be used as part of a course of training on assertiveness, and could usefully be run after **What if?** and followed by **Another perspective, Be prepared** and/or **Dress rehearsal**.

Objectives By the end of this activity participants will:

- have identified areas of their lives where they would like to be more assertive;
- have appraised their present patterns of behaviour;
- have begun to consider alternative approaches which might improve possible outcomes;
- have prioritized areas for practising and demonstrating assertion skills.

Resources Copy of Exercise Sheets 1 and 2 for each participant, pens/pencils. (*Optional*) – Copies of **What if?** Exercise Sheet.

Time The first part of this activity is best completed in participants' own time – overnight, or between sessions for example. Thereafter, 30–45 minutes will be needed.

Method

Step 1: Explain the first part of the activity Participants will be issued with an Exercise Sheet which they are to complete in their own time. This is because some thought needs to go into its completion. There are three columns on the sheet. Column A asks participants to list 10 situations in which they would like to behave more assertively. (If this activity follows **What if?** participants will already have a clearer idea of the areas of their lives which cause them difficulties. Reference can be made to the **What if?** Exercise Sheet.) They should consider all aspects of their lives, working and social. There is space for 10 situations to be recorded.

In column B, participants should identify their usual behaviour pattern in the given situation. For example, if one of the problem areas is 'I need to assert my authority with one difficult member of my team', in column B existing behaviour could be 'I avoid confrontation; I'll lose my cool' or 'I leave things as they are, hoping things will improve'.

In column C participants will identify what sort of behaviour they are presently exhibiting – aggressive, manipulative or passive. In the above situation, avoiding confrontation because of fear of losing control masks aggressive behaviour (although doing nothing is in itself passive). The latter example suggests non-assertive/passive behaviour (although if the person in the given situation drops hints about the team member's behaviour, or suggests dissatisfaction through body language, then the behaviour could be seen as manipulative).

There is not space to record too much detail in columns A and B. Participants should be as concise as possible, but will be able to enlarge on each situation later, during group discussion.

Step 2: Issue Exercise Sheet 1 Clarify any points about procedure and explain when the completed sheets will next be worked on in a training session.

Step 3: Explain and run the next stage in the activity Now that Exercise Sheet 1 has been completed by all participants, they will work in pairs/small groups (trainer's choice) to discuss the entries. Participants should share more detail about situations where they would like to become more assertive, giving examples of present behaviour, and how they think they might progress; and offer advice to colleagues on their problem areas (15–30 minutes).

Step 4: Reconvene the main group; lead a short plenary discussion Ask participants if they would like to share anything from their small group discussion, with the main group.

Step 5: Issue and explain Exercise Sheet 2 As the final part to this activity, working individually, participants should prioritize their problem situations and enter them against the appropriate number on their 'Ladder of success' diagram. The easiest situation to tackle should be entered against number 1, the bottom rung of the ladder, and the other situations recorded in ascending order of difficulty.

This Exercise Sheet is for participants' own use, and should be used as a personal training programme. Individuals will 'climb the ladder' gradually, tackling each situation in sequence, starting with the easiest. (The sheet can be used by individuals as an assertiveness 'life plan' and/or during group training sessions. This activity could usefully be followed by **Be prepared** or **Dress rehearsal**).

Step 6: Sum up, then close the activity by referring to the objectives Identifying, clarifying and prioritizing problem areas is the first step towards actively changing behaviour patterns – or to use the symbolism of the activity, like getting the ladder out of the shed and setting it firmly against a high wall. To climb the ladder safely, one rung at a time should be attempted. Anyone suffering from vertigo will know that even the first rung can be difficult; getting to the top is a real challenge. *You should feel safe and secure on each rung before attempting to climb further.*

Assertiveness training will take individuals through this process, encouraging, supporting and advising as each new challenge is met.

EXERCISE SHEET 1

Ladder of success

In column A explain as succinctly as you can, 10 situations where you would like to be more assertive. Then, in column B, write in your present behaviour in that situation. Finally, in column C, record whether your present behaviour tends to be passive, aggressive, or manipulative.

A	B	C
1.		
2.		
3.		

4.		
5.		
6.		
7.		
8.		
9.		
10.		

EXERCISE SHEET 2

Ladder of success

Climbing the assertiveness ladder – my own training programme

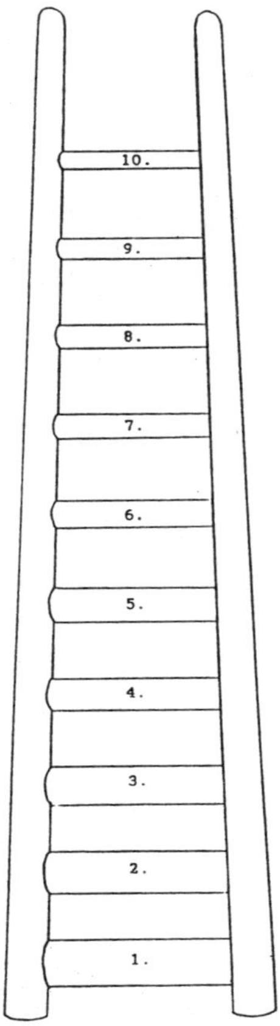

ANOTHER PERSPECTIVE

In a difficult encounter, our own feelings and emotions often override a consideration of the other person's viewpoint. It is useful to try and see the problem areas from the perspective of the other person in the interaction. Although this activity can stand alone, and is a useful exercise in interpersonal skills, it can form part of a structured course preceded by **What if?** and **Ladder of success,** and followed by **Be prepared** and **Dress rehearsal**.

Objectives By the end of this activity participants will:

- be more aware of why communication breakdowns have occurred in the past;
- have identified their own needs, expectations and feelings in a given situation;
- have discussed the other person's perspective with at least one other course member;
- have helped at least one other course member to see their problem situation from the perspective of the other person.

Resources One copy of the Exercise Sheet for each participant, pens/ pencils.

Time 1½ hours.

Method

Step 1: Explain the activity The activity will give everyone the opportunity to analyse either a situation which has caused, or is causing, difficulty, and where they would like to be more assertive, or a problem which has yet to be faced and may cause difficulties unless handled in an assertive way. It is one stage in the preparation for the real-life encounter.

If this activity is preceded by **Ladder of success** participants should choose a situation from their own training programme – preferably the first and easiest option. Remind the group that they should always begin with something small and not too complex, which has a realistic chance of success, and which is not too threatening for them.

During the activity participants will work both individually, and in pairs (one triad if there is an odd number), to evaluate their own and the other person's wants, feelings, needs and expectations in the given situation.

Step 2: Divide group into pairs. Issue Exercise Sheet and pen/pencil to each participant Instruct participants to paraphrase their problem situation and complete Part A of the Exercise Sheet. Explain that time checks will be given so that they will know when to move on to different stages of the activity.

Step 3: Inform participants that they have 10 minutes to discuss each person's situation, putting 'meat on the bones' so that their partner has a fair idea of the problems involved They should try to 'set the scene' for their partner, and give some indication of the relationship with, and the character/behaviour traits of, the other person.

Step 4: Check with pairs that they have had enough time – renegotiate if necessary, and possible. Move on to the next stage Instruct participants to complete Part B of their Exercise Sheet (15 minutes). They should do this without consulting their partner. Participants should be as objective as possible in their responses. This is relatively easy in completing the left-hand 'I' columns, but not so easy when trying to discern what the other person might be feeling or needing from the situation. Participants will have to make an educated guess founded on hard evidence, assumptions based on knowledge of the other person (how they usually react), and their experience of human nature in general – in other words, putting themselves in the other's shoes for a while.

N.B. Stress to participants that this 'evidence' will need to be checked out during the 'real' interaction, while trying to tease out the issues involved in the problem, and finding mutually agreeable and acceptable solutions.

Step 5: Circulate to ensure that participants are keeping their observations specific and objective Under 'What I want' should be written an objective goal, eg 'I want Bill to consult me before making decisions which affect the whole team'. Against 'What I feel' should be listed emotions/feelings about the situation, eg 'I am angry with myself for appearing weak.' In the 'What I need' section should be something like 'I want Bill to consult me and not undermine my authority.' In 'My expectations' should be recorded what is expected when Bill is confronted with his unacceptable behaviour, eg 'He'll come up with all sorts of excuses, so I'll back down again.'

Step 6: When participants have completed Part B of their Exercise Sheet, ask them to swap sheets with their partner(s) Everyone should now have their partner's Exercise Sheet, and working alone, should complete Part C of the Exercise *using their perceptions of their partner's situation.* They should put themselves in the shoes of the person who was, or is going to be, on the receiving end of their partner's communication. If you were that other person, what do you think their wants, feelings, needs and expectations would be in the given situation? Allow 10 minutes for this.

Step 7: Finally, instruct participants to swap sheets again They should discuss discrepancies between their own observations about the other party's needs and so on, and their partner's thoughts on the issue. It is very likely that the other person will be able to project a dimension on the situation not previously considered by the 'owner' of the problem. The feasibility of these perceptions can be analysed, and different approaches to the problem discussed.

Participants should consider ways in which expected outcomes might be improved, and how stereotypical behaviour, on both sides, might be modified.

Step 8: Reconvene the main group for a discussion of the issues raised Ask for general observations.

Questions you might use:

- In what ways was it useful to analyse the situation from both viewpoints?
- In many situations where there is a conflict of interests or ideas, both party's views centre around the self. How useful is it to use this suggested format?

- How helpful was it to see your problem from another, outsider's perspective?
- Have you considered that the other person might behave differently from the stereotypical behaviour you expect of them – especially if you don't conform to what they expect of you?
- What are the benefits of following a procedure similar to the one in the activity before embarking on a difficult interaction?
- Can you see any disadvantages?
- What have you learned from this activity?

Step 9: Sum up, then close the activity by referring to the objectives
Some forethought is important before embarking on a difficult interaction. It is so easy to let emotions rule, to rush into the situation and end up antagonizing the other person, or doing all the things you promised yourself you wouldn't! The results of such an exchange will inevitably be counter-productive. It is also very easy – and human – to see things purely from your own perspective, but assertiveness involves considering the other person's needs as well as your own.

The process of writing lists under the headings suggested (*a*) clarifies the situation, (*b*) establishes previous behaviour patterns on both sides which contribute to blockages, and (*c*) enables progress by seeing the problem as one which can be solved by improved communication and empathy with the other's wants, feelings, needs and expectations.

EXERCISE

Another perspective

Part A

Summarize below either a situation which has caused/is causing you difficulties, or an encounter which you intend to have which could prove troublesome.

____

____

____

Part B

I want:

I feel:

I need:

My expectations are:

(Insert the name of the other person over the dots)

.... wants:

.... feels:

.... needs:

..............................'s expectations are:

Part C *(To be completed by your partner)*

You now know a little about your colleague's situation and what blockages she/he is likely to encounter when having a conversation with the other person.

Try to put yourself in the other person's shoes. What would you be feeling, expecting or wanting from the conversation? Please enter your views below.

If I were .... I would want:

If I were .... I would feel:

If I were .... I would need:

If I were .... my expectations would be:

BE PREPARED

How often do we have conversations in our minds – 'I'll say this, then she'll say that, so I'll respond by...' etc. While not advocating this approach, it is useful to plan for a difficult encounter by having our opening words prepared and rehearsed. It gets us off to a confident start, knowing that our opening gambit, at least, will benefit from an assertive choice of words and phrases with which we feel comfortable. This activity gives participants the opportunity to 'script' the opening lines to a potentially troublesome encounter they plan to have in the future. It could usefully be followed by **Dress rehearsal.**

Objectives By the end of this activity participants will:

- have chosen how to assertively initiate a potentially difficult conversation;
- have had the opportunity to discuss, adjust and refine these opening lines with advice from colleagues;
- have given feedback to other group members;
- have rehearsed the lines in a supportive environment.

Resources Paper and pen/pencil for each participant, copy of the Handout for each participant.

Time 1 hour to 1½ hours.

Method

Step 1: Explain the activity, the procedure and timings Participants should have a particular, real-life situation in mind where they would like to behave assertively. (If this activity is being run as part of a sequence – preceded by **Ladder of success** and/or **Another perspective**, they can practise the first of the situations identified in their training plan.)

Participants will compose their opening words in the given situation. This is assuming one important aspect of assertiveness: the willingness to initiate a potentially difficult conversation.

Initially, participants will work alone on their scripts for about 15 minutes. Then they will share their attempts with others, in small groups, and give and receive advice on how to improve the phraseology and so on (15–30 minutes). Finally, each participant will have the opportunity to rehearse their opening words, again with the opportunity for giving and receiving constructive feedback (15–30 minutes).

Step 2: Issue and go through the Handout Field any questions which may arise.

Step 3: Divide the group into sub-groups of 3 or 4 people Although working individually to begin with, participants who find difficulty in expressing themselves in writing may find it helpful to have the support of colleagues from the outset.

Step 4: Issue paper and pens/pencils and set the groups to work They should use the Handout as a guide, but use words and phrases which come naturally to them, and which follow normal speech patterns. Remind them to consider the person to whom they are going to be saying this, in real-life, and use language appropriate to that person and the situation.

Step 5: After about 15 minutes, suggest that participants begin to discuss and refine their scripts with the help of colleagues They should remember to keep their scripts as short, concise and objective as possible.

Step 6: When participants are happy with their scripts, they can begin to rehearse their words, aloud, within their group After one or two readings of the words, participants should abandon their scripts and rehearse the words paying more attention to tone of voice, eye contact, nervous mannerisms and so on. Individuals may feel happier if they have a 'prompt' to work from – a rough outline which leaves room for a little improvization.

Circulate, offering advice. Encourage group members to give each other constructive feedback.

Step 7: Reconvene the main group; sum up the activity This activity provides a formula which can be used to give you a powerful opening to any interpersonal exchange. Obviously, you won't have a prompt sheet in front of you when you actually deliver the lines in real-life, but writing and rehearsing in this way can give a boost to your confidence, and get the interaction off to an assertive start.

Step 8: Close the activity, referring to the objectives

HANDOUT

Be prepared

When deciding what your opening words are going to be in a potentially difficult interaction, the most important thing to bear in mind is the need to keep it brief and to the point. In this way, the other person is less likely to 'switch off' or interrupt.

You need an opening which is going to capture their attention; which states clearly and objectively what it is you need to discuss (no waffle or irrelevancies), and the problem as you see it. While acknowledging their feelings and needs, you should leave the other person in no doubt about your own feelings, what you want to happen and the consequences if this does (or doesn't) happen. Don't promise or threaten anything if you can't follow through, however.

You will also need to use words and phrases which are easily understood, unambiguous and not too emotive. Talk about facts – about the here and now – not about what you *think* is happening or past behaviour and incidents (unless they have direct bearing on the issue in hand).

Example 1

One of your team, still working her probationary period, is an excellent worker and has fitted in well with her colleagues. However, her timekeeping is poor.

'Mary, I need to talk to you. While I'm very satisfied with your work and how you have fitted in here, during the last month you've been late for work on six occasions.

'I know you've problems with your child-minder, and have been prepared to make up the time, but I would like you to be at your desk by 8.30am, every day, from now on.

'If your timekeeping improves, I will recommend your full-time appointment be confirmed in one month's time. Any more lateness, and at best your probationary period will have to be extended.'

Example 2

Your partner is quite prepared to feed the cat, but always leaves the dirty fork and empty tin on the work surface for you to clear.

'I'd like to talk to you about feeding Moggy. During the past week you've fed him four times and each time left the dirty fork and empty can for me to clear.

'I'm getting irritated with this, and although I'm grateful to you for feeding him if you're first home, I would appreciate it if you would clear up after you.'

DRESS REHEARSAL

This activity offers a format for skills practice, which involves the whole group. It can usefully be run as the final activity of a series beginning with **What if?** and **Ladder of success.** It is the culmination of the preparatory work undertaken by individuals on their own assertiveness programme suggested by these activities. Alternatively, it can be used as a stand-alone activity on role-play.

Objectives By the end of this activity participants will:

- have rehearsed/observed a real-life situation in as realistic a way as is possible in the training room;
- have given/been given constructive criticism and feedback.

Resources (*Optional*) – Copy of participants' scripts from **Be prepared'**; 'props' as required to add authenticity to rehearsals.

Time 45 minutes minimum. Time will depend on how many replays are run, how many participants' situations are rehearsed, and so on.

Method

Step 1: Introduce the activity This activity offers a very thorough group approach to rehearsing and practising assertiveness skills. Most people are anxious about acting out problems in front of a group, or feel that the artificiality of the situation makes it an invalid exercise, but rehearsing a real-life situation is really the best way to practise assertiveness skills. It is a means of practising techniques in a supportive environment with the benefit of peer and trainer feedback. If this activity has been preceded by others in the series –

especially **Another perspective** and **Be prepared** – then the experience of this activity should present no difficulty for participants.

Step 2: Decide which participant's situation is to be the subject of the rehearsal During one training session it is unlikely that more than a couple of situations can be rehearsed, so it is important that the group choose one or two that will be of general interest and scope. If preceded by other activities in the series – especially **Another perspective** and **Be prepared** – participants should choose to follow up a situation previously worked on.

(If used as a stand-alone activity, participants should identify a real-life situation which is not too complex or risky – perhaps a current situation where the 'owner' of that problem would benefit from advice and feedback.)

Step 3: Explain how the rehearsal is to be staged The rehearsal needs to be as realistic as is possible within the limitations imposed by the training situation – hence the title, **Dress rehearsal.** To aid this realism, the 'owner' of the problem, who will rehearse her/his situation in front of the group, should choose a suitable part of the training room, furnish it with whatever props are available, and talk the group through the scene so that they have a clearer picture in their minds' eye. For example, if the setting is an office, the 'owner' could describe where the windows and doors are, what equipment or furniture there is; where colleagues would be sitting and so on.

The 'owner' of the situation to be rehearsed will obviously practice her or his approach to the problem, but will choose a colleague to act out the part of the other person in the encounter. If this activity follows others in the suggested series, it may be useful to choose someone already familiar with the situation to be rehearsed.

Step 4: Ask the 'owner' to give the group a quick resume of the situation to be rehearsed It helps the group, and especially the participant who is to play the other person in the encounter, if details such as the appearance and character of the other person are described. Additional touches can be given, such as words and phrases habitually used or body language displayed.

Step 5: Begin the rehearsal Remind the rest of the group that they are to observe critically so that constructive feedback and advice can be given to the 'owner'.

Let the rehearsal run for as long as is necessary for the two 'players' to get into the exercise, and for the rest of the group to have a general picture of how the 'owner' is handling the situation.

Step 6: Take feedback from the 'players' and the group First, ask the 'owner' how they felt the rehearsal went.

Questions you might use:

- What did you handle well?
- What, if anything, did you find difficult to deal with?
- Is there anything about your approach that you would change?
- Is there anything ... (the other person) could do to make the situation more realistic for you?

Next, ask 'the other person' their views.

Questions you might use:

- What did ... (the 'owner') say or do which you found effective?
- What might ... (the 'owner') have done differently?

Finally, ask the group for their observations. Encourage them to be as specific as possible.

Questions you might use:

- How effective were the 'owner's' opening lines?
- Did content and body language match?
- Was good eye contact and appropriate facial expression maintained?
- What about tone of voice?
- How did the 'other person' respond to the 'owner's' words and actions?
- What went particularly well for the 'owner'?
- How might the 'owner' become even more effective and assertive?

Step 7: Add any observations of your own.* (Optional) *– Set up the first replay The next two stages are optional and depend on the thoroughness you require; whether time allows more than one replay; whether you feel the need for others in the group to rehearse their personal situations and so on.

It is sometimes helpful for the 'owner' of a problem to see their situation rehearsed by others. Although the rehearsal will inevitably

lack some authenticity, at least the 'owner' will see that there are alternative behaviours available to her or him.

Ask for a volunteer to play the 'owner' in a re-run of the situation. Rehearse the situation again. Take feedback from the 'players' and group as before.

Step 8:* (Optional) *Replay the situation with the original 'players' It is important that feedback to the 'owner' is specific, positive and encouraging, emphasizing improvements in her/his assertiveness skills.

Step 9: Thank group for their support and participation. Close the activity

CHAPTER 3

SELF-AWARENESS

CONSEQUENCES

An activity to be run early in a course on assertiveness to identify the effects on self and others of non-assertive behaviour.

Objectives By the end of this activity participants will:

- have identified the possible effects of our behaviour on others;
- have discussed why non-assertive behaviour is bad for health and well-being.

Resources Flipchart and marker.

Time 15–30 minutes.

Method
Step 1: Head a sheet of flipchart paper 'EFFECT ON OTHERS' – Passive behaviour Get the group to suggest ways in which passive behaviour might affect other people. List these on flipchart paper. (See **Trainer's notes**).

Step 2: Repeat the exercise, looking at the effect of aggressive and then manipulative behaviour choices (See **Trainer's notes** for suggestions.)

Step 3: Next, head a flipchart sheet 'EFFECT ON SELF'. Discuss and list the consequences for our own health, well-being, state of mind etc., when we exhibit passive, aggressive and manipulative behaviour (See **Trainer's notes** for suggestions.)

Step 4: Sum up, then close the activity Assertiveness is a behaviour choice. This activity has shown the benefits of choosing assertive behaviour in the majority of cases. If we do not, relationships are likely to suffer, as is our own emotional and physical health.

In an assertive interaction, the other person will have felt comfortable with the communication – at ease and not threatened, challenged or put down. You will have respected their needs, feelings and opinions while not abandoning your own. You will have treated the other as competent and capable in their own right while still feeling good about yourself, your abilities and attributes – a 'WIN/WIN' situation.

TRAINER'S NOTES

Consequences

EFFECTS OF BEHAVIOUR CHOICES ON OTHERS

Aggressive

Aggression can provoke aggression or hostility; situations can then escalate and get out of control; relationships suffer.

Aggression produces resentment or non-co-operation.

The other person may feel angry, defensive, hurt, humiliated, demoralised, demotivated – even fearful.

Passive

People may feel sorry for, or protective towards, you (although they may eventually get exasperated).

Passivity can initiate annoyance.

The other person may feel guilty that they can manipulate or take advantage of you.

The other person can feel irritated, angry, resentful; they can cease to respect you; they can restrict or end contact with you.

Manipulative

People can feel annoyed, irritated, cheated, confused, anxious, or guilty.

EFFECTS OF BEHAVIOUR CHOICES ON SELF

Aggressive

Can give you an initial 'buzz' (but ultimately will not win friends and influence people).

Feeling of release of tension – letting off steam – but at what cost in terms of raised blood pressure.

Can feel disgusted with self – especially in retrospect.

Lowers self-esteem

Churns up digestive system – can cause indigestion, ulcers and worse.

Can cause physical symptoms such as headaches – even heart attacks.

Anger with self at losing control.

Passive

Lowers self-esteem. This can become a downward spiral.

Ashamed of self.

Anger at self and others.

Blaming others for own perceived inadequacies.

Depression.

Confidence declines.

Negative self talk produces self-fulfilling prophecies.

Anxiety, panic attacks, stress related illnesses.

I AM...

An activity which is especially useful on a course where participants are self-nominating, and therefore likely to be individuals lacking in confidence who wish to be more assertive. People who tend toward passive behaviour often have low self-esteem, put the needs of others first, and have difficulty with 'I' statements. This activity encourages participants to look at their personalities, abilities and achievements in a positive light; to take ownership of their attributes, and articulate these qualities.

Objectives By the end of this activity participants will:

- have identified positive personal characteristics, and acknowledged them to the group.

Resources Copy of the Exercise Sheet for each participant, pens/pencils.

Time 1 hour.

Method

Step 1: Introduce the activity Most people find it relatively easy to be self-critical. Individuals who tend most frequently towards passive behaviour often put themselves down – recognize and freely admit to inadequacies and failings, but find it difficult to assert their positive qualities. Society has tended to frown on people who sing their own praises, classifying them as brash or boastful, but continual self-denigration leads to lowered self-esteem and non-assertive behaviour. A balance needs to be found.

Often, too, people who recognize positive qualities in themselves, cannot articulate these in the 'first person'. They cannot say 'I am good at my job' or 'I'm a good cook' but rather 'My boss seems pleased with my work' or 'My husband thinks I'm a good cook'. This often stems from lack of confidence and the need for reassurance. Assertiveness is about developing a confidence in yourself and your own abilities; valuing, and taking ownership of, your own opinions; having a healthy self-respect – without becoming arrogant. It is about making 'I' statements rather than attributing views and opinions to others.

Recognizing and being able to articulate positive traits is an essential step towards becoming more assertive. Practising positive 'I' statements is useful for all manner of activities – contributing to meetings, attending interviews, giving and receiving feedback and so on, as well as for personal and social life.

Step 2: Explain procedure and timings Participants will work alone to complete an Exercise Sheet. They will be asked to complete 'I' statements as set out. Up to 15 minutes can be allowed for this – it is sometimes difficult for people unused to thinking positively about themselves to identify and affirm their qualities. There will follow a plenary session to discuss the exercise.

Step 3: Issue Exercise Sheets, pens/pencils. Begin the exercise Circulate to ensure that individuals are not floundering. It is possible that some, with poor self-image, will have great difficulty in identifying a number of positive qualities.

Step 4: Lead a short discussion on the exercise 'Unpack' the experience. Ask how difficult (or not) people found it. Establish where the difficulties lay. Enquire why some individuals found it hard to identify and acknowledge personal positive qualities.

Stress the points made in the introduction – the importance of respect for self as well as others in assertiveness training; of being able to articulate personal positive qualities at work, at home and in social settings.

Step 5: Ask each participant to choose one attribute or achievement identified on their Exercise Sheet, and to tell the group about it using 'I' statements Choose participants at random rather than going round the circle in a systematic way.

It may be that the individual will need to read their statement until

comfortable with it, but eye contact with the group while saying, for example, 'I am a loyal friend' or 'I am proud of the fact that…' is an important step forward and should be practised. Once they have made their 'I' statement in an assertive way, ask the participant to amplify their assertion. Advise on body language, tone of voice and so on. Encourage the group to join in giving constructive feedback.

Step 6: Ensure that every participant has achieved the goal – to articulate a personal, positive quality in an assertive way. Thank everyone for participating. Close the activity

EXERCISE SHEET

I am...

Complete the following with a positive statement about a personal quality, attribute or achievement:

I am...

I am...

I am...

I am...

I am...

I can...

I can...

I can...

I can...

I can...

I think...

I think...

I believe...

I believe...

What is your greatest achievement? (Use 'I' statements)

What do you like best about yourself?

WARTS AND ALL

An activity which asks participants to be self-critical, and for once to concentrate on the negative aspects of their characters. It's about knowing yourself 'warts and all', identifying areas about which you can do nothing, areas about which you are reasonably content and/or you wish to remain unchanged, and areas which need to be improved through an assertiveness training programme.

Objectives By the end of this activity participants will:

- have ascertained which perceived faults or characteristics they can do nothing about, or which they are happy to accept;
- be more aware of which of their faults or negative characteristics they wish to work on during the training;
- have had the opportunity, in small groups, to discuss strategies for being more assertive in their chosen areas.

Resources Paper, pens/pencils.

Time 1 hour.

Method
Step 1: Explain the activity 99% of assertiveness training is about being positive – developing a self-image with which you are content; increasing confidence; having a respect for self and others. At first sight, therefore, an activity which asks you to look at all the things you dislike about yourself may seem contradictory. However, true self-awareness is an important element – making an honest evaluation of where you are at present, what are your faults as you and as

others see them, what character traits you wish you could change. Equally important is recognizing those things you don't like about yourself which you can't change. What's the point of banging your head against a brick wall, while still carrying feelings of guilt or inadequacy, when there is absolutely nothing you or anyone else can do about it? Far better to recognize, acknowledge, accept and learn to live with these traits. Often, by being more relaxed about an accepted failing is in itself a way forward to ameliorating that trait or, at least, the negative feelings associated with it.

This activity asks participants to be as honest as possible with themselves, and to identify and list everything they consider faults or failings, negative character traits, and everything they don't like about themselves. They should try to look at their characters from their own perspective, but also consider how others see them.

Step 2: Issue paper and pens/pencils. Begin the activity Circulate, clarifying details on procedure if necessary. Most people find it far easier to list faults and failings than to identify positive aspects of their characters, so you shouldn't need (or attempt) to help with content.

Step 3: After about 10 minutes, or when you consider most participants to have completed fairly substantial lists, explain the next stage in the activity Participants should now go through their lists and underline any item about which they can do nothing. For example if one of the things you don't like about yourself is your height, there is very little which can be done about that apart from wearing lifts in your shoes or stooping, depending on your perspective! Next, put a tick against anything you are prepared to accept or live with. For example, you may get very emotional about cruelty to animals, but feel that you don't want to change that sensitivity to a cause you hold dear. Finally, circle faults, failings and negative behaviour traits which you would like to change, indicating which one aspect you would *most* like to change.

Step 4: When participants have annotated their lists, divide them into sub-groups of 3 or 4 people In small groups participants will now go through their lists, looking at each element in turn. First, the underlined items: is there really nothing which can be done to improve these attitudes, characteristics or failings? To pursue the example given above, if a person is unhappy about her or his height

it could be pointed out that there are many advantages of being tall, or short; that choice of clothes, patterns, or colours can make a person appear shorter, taller, thinner, or more rounded. Group members should offer as many positive aspects as they can to their colleagues. There will, of course, be items on everyone's lists about which they can do nothing. There is no point in losing sleep over these. Acknowledge, accept and learn to like yourself in spite of these traits.

Next, go through the ticked items. If participants are honestly happy to accept a failing, and it gives them no problem to do so, this should not be pursued at any length.

Lastly, groups should look at perceived faults and failings which they would like to change. Group members should offer constructive suggestions about how this change might be achieved.

Throughout, particular attention should be paid to both personally perceived faults and failings, and behaviour which another person considers to be negative in an individual. For example, a participant may identify untidiness as a fault, but this may be because a partner sees them as untidy. Personally, they may not consider it to be a fault. This aspect of the activity is all-important in the context of assertiveness training, because the issue here may not be how to accept untidiness as a (personally) acceptable trait, nor about changing a fault or attitude towards tidiness, but about addressing the issue with the partner.

Stress that individuals need only reveal to others in their group what they want to share with others.

Step 5: Set the groups to work Circulate, offering guidance, and ensuring that feedback to individuals within the group is positive and helping to raise self-esteem, rather that reinforcing negative self-perception.

Step 6: Reconvene the main group for plenary discussion Ask if there is anything individuals would like to share with the main group. Lead a short discussion on areas participants intend to work on during the training – things they don't like about themselves which they intend to change – how they might go about this. To save time, you could just discuss the aspect each would *most* like to change.

Ensure that each participant has something positive to work on before closing the activity.

Step 7: Sum up, then close the activity by referring to the objectives
By taking time out to be honest about all our perceived failings, then eliminating those about which we can do nothing, or which we are prepared to accept, this clears the mind to deal with a self-improvement programme which can be pursued with the help and support of colleagues through assertiveness training.

Participants should keep their lists as reminders, and also as a guide to their own development programme.

EFFECTIVENESS

This is a questionnaire to test the appropriateness of participants' behaviour in given circumstances. It serves to demonstrate that assertiveness is not *always* the best choice. Some situations call for firmer action – others, more reticent behaviour.

Objectives By the end of this activity participants will:

- have identified areas where they are already effective and others where more practice is required;
- better recognize that assertiveness is a *choice* of behaviour;
- have had the opportunity to discuss choosing appropriate behaviours to meet difficult situations.

Resources Copies of the Exercise Questionnaire and Score Sheet for each participant, pens/pencils, flipchart and marker for trainer use.

Time 1½ hours to 2 hours.

Method

Step 1: Introduce the activity The activity is in two parts. Firstly, participants will complete a self-evaluation questionnaire to assess personal effectiveness in given situations. Questionnaires of this sort are often felt to be unsatisfactory because in 'real-life' individual reactions will differ depending on a variety of factors. The second part of the activity addresses this, allowing participants to more accurately assess what would be appropriate responses to each scenario set.

Step 2: Issue the Exercise Questionnaires and pens/pencils. Begin the activity Explain that participants should work alone to complete the questionnaires, and should respond by ticking the box which most closely represents how they would react to the scenarios set, *not* what they think the correct response *should be*. Allow 15 minutes.

Step 3: Issue and explain the Score Sheets Transfer responses onto the Score Sheet. For example, if a participant chose option 2 to the first question (Scenario 1), encircle the 2 in column A, question 1. Column E represents the most effective response in each case, so if the number recorded is the same as the one in column E encircle that number as well. Allow 10 minutes for participants to record and total their scores.

Next, instruct participants to multiply the total number of circles in column E by 5. This will give each participant an effectiveness rating of between 0 and 50.

Step 4: Read out the effectiveness ratings, allowing participants to assess for themselves where their score fits in the range You could flipchart these assessments if you wish. They are as follows:

0– 9 Not effective
10–19 Fairly effective
20–29 Good
30–39 Very effective
40–50 Excellent.

Step 5: Ask participants to share their views on the questionnaire Participants should not be asked to divulge their effectiveness ratings if they do not wish to do so, but it is important to allow participants to 'unpack' their feelings about the exercise itself.

Questions you might use:

- Did your own effectiveness rating surprise you? Why?
- Did you feel the responses offered to the scenarios to be fair ones?
- Was it easy to relate to at least one of the responses offered? Why . . . or why not?
- Were there questions where your response would have been very different from any of those offered?

You should point out (if discussion has not already touched on this) that effective behaviour is about choosing the most appropriate

response to a given situation. This does not necessarily mean an assertive response. Remember that assertiveness is about choice. There will be times in everyone's life when aggression is called for. Equally there will be times when we should choose not to assert ourselves. The scenarios gave instances of both. Effectiveness is shown primarily by the effectiveness scale, but is also indicated by a balance of behaviours indicated by the totals on the Score Sheet.

Step 6: Explain the procedure for the remainder of the activity Because, in most instances, we would all react differently to each scenario depending on the people involved, the background to the situation, and our own feelings at the time – elements which couldn't be written into the questionnaire – participants now have the opportunity to deliberate on each question with colleagues. In small groups, using the scenarios as a basis for discussion, participants will talk about why they responded as they did, offer advice on how inappropriate responses might be modified, suggest why certain behaviours are more appropriate at some times than others, discuss when it pays *not* to be assertive, and so on. Allow 30 minutes for this.

Step 7: Reconvene main group. Take each scenario in turn and ask groups to report on their discussions Point out that the questionnaire could not cover all the range of possible responses. Group discussions may have decided that alternative responses would have been more effective than some of those suggested. This is fine. The questionnaire is intended as a vehicle for discussion – to demonstrate that effective behaviour is not necessarily assertive behaviour. Assertiveness is about choice, and assertiveness training is concerned with choosing and practising *appropriate* responses until they become second nature.

Step 8: Close the activity referring back to the objectives

EXERCISE

Effectiveness

How effective am I? – Self-evaluation questionnaire

Tick the response which best represents how you would react to each situation, *not* what you consider to be the correct response.

Scenario 1

Because you had agreed to organize the raffle for a community event for the past three years, it is assumed, by the committee, that you will run it again this year. You had intended to hand over this duty, so are very annoyed when you see the minutes stating that you will again be responsible. What would you do?

Option 1. Accept things as they are, vowing that you will definitely not arrange the raffle in future years. ☐

Option 2. Telephone the chair of the committee, expressing your feelings about not being consulted, and explaining why you will not be organizing the raffle this year. ☐

Option 3. Wait until the next meeting, then give the committee a piece of your mind, letting them know exactly how you feel about being taken for granted, and refusing to run the raffle again. ☐

Scenario 2

You have been stuck in a traffic jam for ages. The cars ahead of you start to move away; you put your car in gear – and the engine stalls. You turn the ignition key and the engine turns over, but refuses to fire. The driver behind begins to blow his horn. What would you do?

Option 1. Get out of your car and walk back to the driver to say something like 'May I suggest that I sit in your car blowing the horn, while you go and see if you can get my car started!' ☐

Option 2. Acknowledge the other driver with a wave of the hand; switch on the hazard warning lights, and open the bonnet to let others know you have engine failure. ☐

Option 3. Ignore the other drivers, keep your head down, and keep trying to start your engine. ☐

Scenario 3

You are out walking your dog when you see a group of young boys in an alley between houses using spray paint to 'adorn' a wall with graffiti. What would you do?

Option 1. Think to yourself 'It's none of my business', and walk on. ☐

Option 2. Go up to the boys and say 'You are vandalizing someone else's property. I'd like you to stop it at once, and clean up the mess you've made.' ☐

Option 3. Shout out 'Stop that!' Then go and investigate. ☐

Scenario 4

You work in the leisure industry. It is peak season, and the firm is short-staffed because of illness. You had agreed to work an extra day for the last two weeks, but have prior commitments this week. Your boss says to you 'I know this is asking a lot, but the situation with staffing is even worse this week. Will you look after the information desk again this Saturday please?' What would you be most likely to say?

Option 1. 'As you know, I've been more than willing to help out in the past, and I know you've got staffing problems at the moment. I feel awful letting you down, but I've got something planned this weekend.' ☐

Option 2. 'No, I can't. Try Sally; she might help out.' ☐

Option 3. 'Sorry; I've got prior commitments this weekend, so no, I won't be able to work on Saturday.' ☐

Scenario 5

You and a friend are out shopping. She has to return a faulty item to a shop, so she goes to sort out a refund while you look around another department. As she is a long time, you go to check on her progress. She is in a heated discussion with the person behind the desk, but seems to be in control of the situation. What would you do?

Option 1. Go to see if you can offer your friend some support to bring the situation to a favourable conclusion. ☐

Option 2. Leave them to sort it out. ☐

Option 3. Intervene, telling the shop assistant that if he doesn't give an immediate refund, you will call the manager. ☐

Scenario 6

The firm you work for is in financial difficulties, and there have been rumours of redundancies. Morale is low, and your boss, in particular, is obviously stressed. He has been moody and short tempered recently although normally he is a fair and reasonable man. Today he criticises you – unjustly, but loudly and at length – for a minor error made by one of your staff. What would be your most likely response?

Option 1. 'In the circumstances, I'll ignore your remarks! You're obviously not yourself today!' ☐

Option 2. 'You're right; that shouldn't have happened. I'll see to it right away.' ☐

Option 2. 'I'm sorry, those items should have been checked. However, you're wrong to say that I'm careless. My standards and those of my team are high. Mistakes sometime happen.' ☐

Scenario 7

When you can spare the time, you visit an elderly, housebound neighbour. Because she has so few visitors, she tends to use delaying tactics to keep you in the house for as long as possible. You have to allow for this in deciding how long you can stay! Today, you really are in a dash, but call in to check that she is OK. You tell her you are in a hurry and can't stay, but she still keeps you for a chat; then at the front door she says 'Oh I forgot. The light bulb has blown in my bathroom. Could you just put in a new one for me before you go?' What would you do?

Option 1. Say 'Of course. Show me where you keep your spare bulbs, and I'll do that for you. Then I really must go.' ☐

Option 2. Suggest that she keeps the bathroom door open and use the light cast from the landing until you've got time to change the bulb for her. ☐

Option 3. Say firmly, 'No. As I explained, I've got to go now. I'll change the bulb for you when I've got more time – this evening perhaps.' ☐

Scenario 8

Money is tight, so you have decided to confine donating to those charities you feel most worthy. This is fine in principle, until the doorbell rings and on the doorstep is a collector for a charity you have decided not to support. What would you do?

Option 1. Decide to have baked beans instead of a chop, and give the usual amount. ☐

Option 2. Explain that you have to restrict your support to just one or two favourite charities, so reluctantly can't give a donation at this time. ☐

Option 3. Grudgingly give a few pence just to get rid of the collector, ensuring that you collect a stick-on badge to wear so that you won't be pestered again. ☐

Scenario 9

You and a friend are travelling home from an evening at the theatre. There is just one other person in the underground carriage. At the next stop a group of youths, rather noisy and drinking from lager cans, get into your carriage. One of them gets out a packet of cigarettes, and is fumbling around in his jacket pocket – presumably for a lighter. What do you do?

Option 1. Glower at the group and say loudly to your friend 'I hope he isn't going to start smoking in here!' ☐

Option 2. Ignore the situation – try to ignore the group of youths all together – and continue with your private conversation. ☐

Option 3. Smile at the potential offender, and remind him politely but firmly of the No Smoking rules on the London Underground. ☐

Scenario 10

It is the middle of the night. You are woken by the sound of a woman screaming for help. You look out of the window and see a man and woman arguing in the street. He is shaking and pushing her, and as you watch, he actually strikes her. What would you do?

Option 1. Phone for the police, then go down and try and reason with the man. ☐

Option 2. Open the window and shout 'I've sent for the police; now leave her alone.' ☐

Option 3. Think, 'It's their problem; don't get involved' and try to go back to sleep. ☐

SCORE SHEET

Effectiveness

Circle the option you chose for each of the scenarios, on the grid below. For example, if you decided option 2 would be closest to your response to scenario 1, encircle 2 in column A. If the number you selected is the same as the number in column E, encircle that as well.

Scenarios	*A*	*P*	*AG*	*E*
1	2	1	3	2
2	2	3	1	2
3	2	1	3	3
4	3	1	2	3
5	1	2	3	2
6	3	2	3	3
7	3	1	2	1
8	2	1	3	2
9	3	2	1	2
10	1	3	2	2
Totals	____	____	____	____

Add up each column. Effective behaviour will show a balanced score. Too many in column A may prove that you choose assertive behaviour to the detriment of the feelings or well-being of others, for example; or too many in column P may indicate you neglect your own needs.

I'LL ASSERT MYSELF IF . . .

As the name suggests, this activity asks participants to consider times when they can be assertive with relative ease, and times when the situation demands an assertive response. It goes on to look at barriers to assertive behaviour – what inner messages prevent assertive action.

Objectives By the end of this activity participants will:

- recognize that everyone can be, and is, assertive on occasions;
- have discussed areas where self-doubt blocks assertive behaviour;
- have looked at ways of overcoming barriers to assertiveness.

Resources Paper and pens/pencils for each participant, flipchart and marker, copy of the Handout for each participant, copy of **Trainer's notes**.

Time 1 hour.

Method
Step 1: Explain the first part of the activity Working in small groups of 3 or 4 people, participants will make a list headed 'I'll assert myself if . . .' giving all the reasons why they are confident and happy being assertive, and also times when they feel obliged to assert themselves (10 minutes).

Step 2: Divide the group into smaller groups of 3 or 4. Issue paper and pens/pencils. Set the groups to work If they need help getting started, offer one or two suggestions from the handout.

Step 3: After about 10 minutes, or when groups have run out of ideas, reconvene the main group. Write up a composite list on the flipchart Discuss each item as it is written up. Where relevant, ask whether the inclusion is a group observation or the experience of one person. Ask for examples to illustrate inclusions. Involve the whole group in these discussions.

Step 4: Issue the Handout Explain that this is a list taken from observations of previous assertiveness training groups. To make it a more personal handout, participants can add any of their observations, not included, in the space provided. Point out that the corollary of all these statements is where the dangers lie; eg I won't assert myself if . . . I'm not feeling good about myself . . . or . . . if I can't be sure of the outcome.

Step 5: Head up a flipchart sheet 'Wouldn't it be awful if . . .'. Ask participants to call out all the kinds of negative self-talk which prevents assertive behaviour Compile a flipchart list, including the suggestions in the **Trainer's notes** if these are not suggested by the group.

Step 6: Lead a discussion on the possible consequences if these 'what ifs?' happened Discuss the pros and cons of being assertive in spite of these doubts. What is the best that could happen? What is the worst that could happen? How can these barriers to assertion be overcome?

Step 7: Sum up, then close the activity, referring to the objectives Stress that assertiveness is a choice of behaviour. There will be situations when being assertive is not the correct choice. However, if you are held back because of self-doubt or negative self-talk, you should try to practise more assertive behaviour. Old Chinese saying – *'He that is afraid to shake the dice will never throw a six.'*

HANDOUT

I'll assert myself if...

I'll assert myself if...

- I am feeling on top of things
- I am feeling good about myself
- I think the other person can take it
- Principles are involved
- Someone else doesn't do it
- It's on someone else's behalf
- I am sure of my ground
- The status quo can't continue
- I am justified
- I am pushed to my limits
- It's what I *should* feel
- It's with a peer
- It's to a subordinate
- I'll still be liked
- The time is right
- No-one will get angry if I do
- I won't hurt anyone's feelings
- I am sure about what I feel
- I don't feel intimidated by the other person
- It's really going to bug me if I don't
- I can be sure of the outcome
- It's part of my job
- No-one else says what I am thinking
- I can find the right words

- I am sure I won't get emotional
- I can control my anger
- It won't cause a scene
- I have all the facts and information
- I am sure my voice won't shake
- I believe I will 'win'.

Add below any others of your own

- ____________________
- ____________________
- ____________________
- ____________________
- ____________________
- ____________________
- ____________________
- ____________________

TRAINER'S NOTES

I'll assert myself if...

Below are a few suggestions, compiled from participants' lists on assertiveness courses run by the author.

Wouldn't it be awful if...

- I make a mistake
- I clam up
- Our relationship changes
- I am proved wrong
- I am talked into a corner
- My opinion is challenged
- I am made to look stupid
- They get angry with me
- They reject me
- They stop liking me
- They disapprove of me
- They no longer consider me 'nice'
- They won't listen
- I am left out of their circle
- I lose my job
- I lose their friendship
- I am criticized
- I cannot find the words to express myself
- I blush
- I lost control and got really angry
- I cried

AM I MANAGING?

This is a self-test questionnaire for supervisors/junior managers which can be issued early in the course. It will help individuals to clarify their managerial strengths and weaknesses, assess their present level of assertiveness, and identify areas where assertiveness skills might be improved. This will help them to focus their own learning during the course. Little or no processing is involved.

Objectives By the end of this activity participants will:

- have been given the opportunity to evaluate their assertiveness skills as managers;
- recognize where they need to concentrate their efforts during assertiveness skills training.

Resources Copy of the Exercise Questionnaire for each participant.

Time Participants complete the questionnaire in their own time.

Participants Junior managers and staff supervisors.

Method
Step 1: Introduce the activity This questionnaire is a self-evaluation exercise. It is focused on issues relating to managerial style, and should help clarify individuals' assertiveness training goals. The forms will not be collected in; no-one else need see the responses; there will be no plenary discussion unless anyone feels the need to share, with the group, issues resulting from the exercise. The questionnaire should be completed in participants' own time – when they

have a few minutes to carefully consider the questions and appreciate the implication of their responses in terms of training needs.

Step 2: Issue a copy of the Exercise Questionnaire to each participant Inevitably, participants will begin to read the questionnaires as they are distributed to the group, but as soon as every person has a copy, remind them that this activity should be completed either during a break, or sometime out of course hours when individuals can work at their own pace. It is in each person's interest, however, that the questionnaire be completed as soon as possible in order that individual training needs can be recognized and met.

Step 3: Move on to the next session on the course programme

Step 4: (Optional) Later in the course, lead a short discussion of the activity This should not be an in-depth debate – rather a general overview of the activity.

Questions you might use:

- Has everyone found time to consider the issues raised in the questionnaire?
- Was it helpful? In what way? (or why not?).
- Has it clarified your self-assessment in terms of training needs?
- Were some questions more difficult than others to answer with a yes/no response? Which were they? Why was that?
- Have you established areas where it would serve you and others best to modify your present behaviour?
- Is there any area where you are not prepared or willing to modify your behaviour, although you now recognize it to be unassertive? Why?
- What areas of assertiveness training would most help you manage more effectively?

SELF-EVALUATION QUESTIONNAIRE

Am I managing?

Write 'Yes' or 'No', in the right-hand margin, against the following questions.

(1) When you are not sure of something, do you find it easy to ask the help of (*Enter Yes/No*)
- (a) your boss ______
- (b) your staff ______
- (c) your colleagues? ______

(2) Are you able to 'hold your own' with an aggressive or domineering person? ______

(3) If the answer to 2 is 'yes', do you 'hold your own' by matching aggression with aggression – and usually win? ______

(4) If the answer to 2 is 'yes', do you 'hold your own' by staying calm and attempting to moderate the behaviour of the other person? ______

(5) Do you have confidence in your own judgement? ______

(6) Are you able to avoid being manipulated by other people
- (a) boss ______
- (b) staff ______
- (c) colleagues ______
- (d) suppliers/customers? ______

(7) Do you ever pursue an argument, even when you know your point has been made? __________

(8) When someone is being unfair, unjust or aggressive, do you immediately point this out to them? __________

(9) Are you reluctant to discipline your staff? __________

(10) Do you find it difficult to say thank you to staff? __________

(11) Do you often give praise for work well done? __________

(12) When at fault, do you find it easy to apologize to
   - (a) your boss __________
   - (b) your staff __________
   - (c) your colleagues __________
   - (d) suppliers/customers? __________

(13) Are you ever over-apologetic with
   - (a) your boss __________
   - (b) your staff __________
   - (c) your colleagues __________
   - (d) suppliers/customers? __________

(14) Can you behave assertively when a boss or colleague interferes? __________

(15) Do you ever undertake unpleasant tasks yourself rather than delegate? __________

(16) Do you ever keep enjoyable tasks which could or should be delegated? __________

(17) Do you feel that sometimes you are taken advantage of by
   - (a) your boss __________
   - (b) your staff __________
   - (c) your colleagues? __________

(18) Can you give constructive feedback to
   - (a) your boss __________
   - (b) your staff __________
   - (c) your colleagues? __________

(19) Can you accept justified criticism? __________

(20) Do you encourage personal feedback from
   (a) your boss ________
   (b) your staff ________
   (c) your colleagues? ________

(21) When a member of staff makes a request you feel is unreasonable, do you find it easy to refuse? ________

(22) If the answer to 21 is 'yes', do you feel the situation has had a mutually successful outcome, ie no hard feelings? ________

(22) If the answer to 21 is 'no', do you feel that your authority has suffered? ________

(23) If a member of staff makes a reasonable request, but you can't comply, do you feel guilty? ________

(24) If one of your staff does a job badly, do you ask for it to be done correctly? ________

(25) Do you ever prefer to amend poor work yourself
   (a) because it's quicker to do so ________
   (b) to avoid a confrontation? ________

(26) Do you find staff appraisals difficult to manage? ________

(27) Do you worry if you have to write a poor appraisal report on one of your staff? ________

(28) Do you give staff sufficient opportunity to express ideas and help in problem-solving and decision-making processes? ________

(29) Are you ever guilty of over-control – at meetings with your staff for example? ________

(30) Do you consider yourself part of the organizational team? ________

When you have considered all the questions above and indicated your response by writing yes or no in the right-hand margin, go through the list again and indicate in the left-hand margin those areas with which you are dissatisfied, or where you feel there could be improvement in your managerial skills. It is to these elements of assertiveness training that you should concentrate your efforts.

BODY TALK

A simple activity whereby participants practise using good posture and positive body language.

Objectives By the end of this activity participants will:

- have experienced the difference between body language which gives a negative impression to others, and body language which projects a positive self-image;
- have received and given feedback to other group members on personal effectiveness through good posture and body language.

Resources None.

Time 30–45 minutes.

Method

Step 1: Introduce the activity by giving a short input on the differences between basic passive and aggressive body language, and an assertive image (See **Trainer's notes/Handout.**)

Step 2: Explain the procedure for the first part of the activity Participants will be divided into groups of 3 or 4 people. They should imagine that they have just entered their doctor's consulting room, or been summoned to their boss's office, or called for interview – any formal situation. Each will take it in turn to first adopt negative body language while in a sitting position. First, try using passive, defensive body language. Next, still sitting, try to assume aggressive, arrogant postures. Colleagues can help by suggesting other ways body language might show passivity or aggression. Then the same group

member should just sit naturally – as she or he would normally sit in such a situation – and get feedback from the group about what messages are being conveyed by their body language. Finally, with the help and advice of other group members, individuals will get into a sitting position which appears relaxed, open, comfortable *and assertive.* Each group member will practise all four stages.

Step 3: Begin the activity Ensure that each group member has the chance to practise and receive feedback and advice from colleagues.

Step 4: Take feedback from the group Ask for comments or observations. Field any questions.

Step 5: Explain and run the second part of the activity Repeat the whole exercise, *standing* this time. Participants should imagine they are in a potentially stressful situation – perhaps talking to an important client, or in a shop complaining about a faulty purchase.

Step 6: When everyone has had the chance to practise standing assertively, reconvene the main group for a short discussion of the learning points Ask for observations from the group.

Questions you might use:

- What negative poses do you habitually assume?
- What assertive, positive signals do you habitually send to others?
- How can you minimize negative body language?
- Why do you think it's important to project an assertive image through body language?
- What have you learned from this activity?

Step 7: Sum up, then close the activity. Issue the Handout With practice, you will be able to adopt a relaxed, confident, open posture at will – however difficult the situation. By consciously relaxing the shoulders and muscles of the face, standing tall, adopting an open stance – without appearing too laid back – your confidence will be given the boost it needs to tackle any situation in an assertive manner.

TRAINER'S NOTES/HANDOUT

Body talk

It would be unreasonable to expect everyone to stand or sit in an assertive way – all the time. We can all slump in front of the television, or adopt an ultra-open, laid back pose when relaxing with friends. That's perfectly normal and okay.

What this activity is aiming to achieve is an awareness of posture, bearing, gesture which conveys nervousness, anxiety, irritation, anger and so on, so that these attitudes can be avoided in situations which require assertiveness.

By learning, memorizing and practising an assertive bearing, both sitting and standing, these positions can be adopted, naturally, when the need arises. Posture will improve, confidence will grow – you will more easily become the assertive person which your image is projecting.

Think about the following:

Posture Do you look relaxed and confident? Are you assuming an 'open' posture? Are you exhibiting any unnecessary crossing gestures? (tightly folded arms for example). Are you standing/sitting in an upright or slouched position? Are your shoulders hunched or tense? Do you 'lock' your knees when standing? Is your weight evenly distributed to both feet and legs?

Distance Are you a comfortable distance from the other person? Are you in danger of either invading their personal space, or being too far away to seem approachable/friendly/confident? Are you standing/sitting at a suitable angle to the other person? ('Head on' positions can appear confrontational, for example.)

Environment Are you both sitting or both standing? If seated, are your chairs of similar design and height?

Eyes Are you maintaining appropriate eye contact when both talking and listening? Is your expression relaxed and friendly?

Mouth and jaw Do you jut your jaw forward when speaking? Are you clenching your teeth or holding your jaw tightly? What expression does your mouth convey? Is your smile appropriate?

Face Are your face muscles relaxed? Do you frown? Squint? Scowl?

Gestures Do your hands twitch or flutter nervously? Do you clench your fists? Are you forever touching parts of your face as you communicate? Do you fidget, or fiddle with pens, jewellery, hair? Do you fold arms tightly or twine legs around each other? Do you shift from foot to foot? Do you indulge in finger strumming or foot tapping? Do you examine your finger nails, nibble at fingers or pick bits of imaginary fluff from your clothes?

Cultural differences

Be aware of cultural differences. This is a vast topic – and a very interesting one. Signs, gestures, posture, body language can mean different things to different people in different parts of the world. For example, socially acceptable spacial distances differ from culture to culture. It has even been suggested that people born and brought up in cities can stand closer to each other without feeling uncomfortable than can those born in rural areas. Similarly, the British seem to prefer sitting or standing at right angles to each other in conversation. Other cultures favour different stances.

You will find that Asian people tend to use less direct eye contact than most European and North American countries. Asian children are taught to lower the eyes as a mark of respect to the other person.

MIRROR

This activity is about body language, so it should have been preceded by trainer input on this topic; (please see Step 1 below, however). Specifically it looks at how mirroring another's body language – without taking it to extremes, of course – can help establish rapport. This is especially useful when preparing for difficult meetings, counselling, or giving feedback for example.

Objectives By the end of this activity participants will:

- have experienced how mirrored body language can develop a feeling of well-being and rapport with another, while cross-communication – in body language terms – can create unease in both parties.

Resources Copies of **Brief for speakers**, and **Brief for listeners**; and copies of **Handout** (*optional*).

Time 45 minutes to one hour.

Method

Step 1: Explain the procedure for the first part of the activity Do not, at this stage, tell participants that the activity is about body language. It is important that the first part of the activity is performed without the self-consciousness that this awareness would create.

Explain that the group will be divided into pairs, and that one partner will talk about a given topic while the other *actively* listens (making encouraging noises, asking questions for clarification, etc). The conversation should last for about 5 minutes.

Step 2: Divide group into pairs and issue Instruction Sheets Give a topic sheet (Brief for Speakers) to one partner and listening instructions (Brief for Listeners) to the other. If there is an odd number of participants, one person could observe the conversations. Issue that person with a listener's Instruction Sheet. She or he should just observe and not join in the dialogues.

Step 3: Allow participants a few moments to read their instructions and collect their thoughts. Begin the activity Observe the exchanges closely for feedback later.

Step 4: After 5 minutes, ask participants to halt their conversations Explain to the 'speakers' that their partners had instructions to deliberately avoid eye contact; to use negative body language, etc. Ask for reactions from the group. (Ask for feedback from the observer if one was used.)

Questions you might use:

- How easy/difficult was it for the listeners to use obstructive body language? Why?
- Were any of the 'speakers' aware that their partners were being unduly inattentive?
- What signals were being given?
- How did you react?

Step 5: Give some input on positive body language and mirroring Remind participants about eye contact, open posture, active listening and so on. Explain the mirroring theory (see **Trainer's notes/Handout**).

Step 6: Repeat the exercise, only this time the listener should adopt mirroring body language and send positive verbal and non-verbal signals The conversation could continue from where it left off earlier, or a new topic discussed. However, partners should keep the same role – speaker or listener. Ask listeners to actively pursue, but be subtle in, their use of mirroring so that it encourages, but does not distract their partner.

Step 7: After about 5 minutes, ask participants to stop their conversation. Reconvene the main group. Ask for reactions from the group.

Questions you might use:

- Did this conversation seem different from the last one?
- In what way? or Why not?
- What, if anything, did you notice about the tone of voice you used?
- Was the conversation more or less animated this time?
- When would it *not* be a good idea to mirror another's body language?
- If someone is displaying negative body language, how might the mirroring technique be used to good effect?
- How might you use the mirroring technique to good effect in your own working/social life?

Step 8: (Optional) – Issue Trainer's notes as a Handout. Sum up, then close the activity referring to the objectives If necessary, acknowledge the artificiality of the exercise, which had to be a simulation to give participants a feel for mirroring behaviour. Explain the reasons why mirroring can be effective if handled skilfully.

We tend to feel more at home with people who are like us. This could be in appearance – style of dress, apparent lifestyle – or attitude. We can help put the other person at ease, and build rapport, by projecting this 'like us' attitude. This can be helped by mirroring posture, gestures and so on. We should only mirror positive body language of course. There would be little point in mirroring twitchy, nervous mannerisms – both would end up nervous wrecks! The mirroring needs to be subtle – not consciously noticed by the other person – or it could become at best irritating, and at worst, offensive.

INSTRUCTION SHEET: BRIEF FOR SPEAKERS

Mirror

Talk to your partner, for about 5 minutes, on one of the following topics. State your views on the subject as clearly and assertively as you can.

Why foreign holidays are preferable to holidays in your home country.

The benefits of exercise and a healthy diet.

Crime and punishment.

Alternatively, talk on a topic of your own choice.

You have a couple of minutes to think about what you are going to say.

INSTRUCTION SHEET: BRIEF FOR LISTENERS

Mirror

Do not show this Brief to your Partner

Your partner has been asked to share her/his views with you on a given topic.

For the purpose of this part of the exercise, try to use **Obstructive** body language while still participating in the conversation.

For example, look at your partner occasionally, but also let your gaze wander about the room. If your partner is sitting forward, laze back in your chair. If they cross their arms or legs, ensure that yours are uncrossed. You could occasionally fiddle with your cuffs, pick imaginary bits of fluff from your clothes, examine your nails, and so on.

Try not to make this obstructive behaviour too obvious, be subtle – and continue to respond verbally to your partner.

TRAINER'S NOTES/HANDOUT

Mirror

Research has shown that people 'in tune' with each other, unconsciously mirror each other's movements and gestures. Two people, sitting in animated conversation on a topic about which they are in agreement, will probably both be sitting forward in their chairs. If they have crossed their legs, they will have mirrored their companion.

If subsequently an element of contention comes into the conversation, the person who is in disagreement will begin to sit further back in the chair. They may have had (for example) their hands to their faces, or have used them to animate the conversation. As disagreement is felt, the hands may well be clasped in the lap, or the arms folded. The opposite leg will be crossed.

This happens subconsciously, but should give the receiver warning signs that although nothing may yet have been said, there is no longer complete harmony between the two.

You can watch this phenomenon in practice at any meeting. You will see which parties are in agreement with each other by the mirroring which takes place.

To a certain extent, mirroring can be manufactured. Sales people are taught how, by mirroring clients' posture and movement, a rapport can be quickly forged. Obviously, the skill lies in the subtlety of the mirroring. Copying every mannerism and gesture, as it happens, will be quickly detected, and most certainly have the opposite effect to the desired one of friendliness and affinity!

However, used with sensitivity, manufactured mirroring can benefit relationships. It can help to put the other person at ease, and communicate to them on a sub-conscious level, that you are compatible people.

CHAPTER 4

FLASHPOINTS AND BRUISES

BIG BOYS DON'T CRY

Some of the problems associated with lack of assertiveness or aggression can be attributed to learned behaviours. Gender roles are often dictated by conditioning. Although assertiveness training is not so much about causes, as how to deal with the problems they have created, it is useful to look at the subject of conditioning – if only to help alleviate feelings of guilt. In theory, anything which has been learned can be unlearned or modified. Passive or aggressive behaviour can be replaced by assertiveness.

Objectives By the end of this activity participants will:

- have considered how conditioning might influence patterns of behaviour in men and women.

Resources Notepaper, pens/pencils, flipchart paper and marker pens, means of attaching flipchart sheets to the wall, dictionary (*optional*), copy of **Trainer's notes**.

Time 1 hour.

Method

Step 1: Explain the activity This activity considers how conditioning might affect adult behaviour. It looks at how gender roles might be dictated by learned behaviours. It does not attempt to excuse aggressive behaviour, or suggest that someone who is passive by nature can do nothing about it. By looking at why we might behave in certain ways – because of our upbringing for example – it prepares the way for modifying unwanted behaviours, and helps alleviate the guilt some of us feel about our unassertive feelings and actions.

Step 2: Explain procedure and timings There will be three groups, each with a slightly different brief. The first group will discuss and list conditioning in girls and boys from pre-birth to starting school – say, at 5 years old. The second group will discuss how conditioning affects girls and boys through their school years, through puberty to adulthood. The third group will consider how language and the media affect our conceptions of gender roles and assertive behaviour.

Groups will have 30–45 minutes to prepare (a time check will be given after half an hour). Each group should nominate a spokesperson who will then present their group's findings. Flipchart paper and markers are available to aid group presentations.

Step 3: Divide the group into three sub-groups and set them to work Issue notepaper and pens/pencils, flipchart paper and markers. (*Optional*) – Give the third group a dictionary. This may help with their brief to look at language. Circulate among groups, helping to get them started if necessary (see **Trainer's notes**).

Step 4: Give a time check after 30 minutes Remind groups that they are to give a presentation. Renegotiate times if necessary.

Step 5: Reconvene the main group. Run the presentations: first the pre-birth to 5 group, then the school to adulthood, finally the language and media group As each group presents, encourage discussion so that lists can be amended and added to.

Step 6: Thank the group for their presentations. Lead a short discussion on the findings Ask for general comments.

Questions you might use:

- Had any of you given this topic much thought before?
- What, if anything, surprised you from these discussions?

- What can you deduce from these discussions?
- In what ways might conditioning lead us to overvalue/undervalue ourselves?
- How might conditioning direct our adult behaviour?
- Do you feel that nature or nurture is responsible for temperament and behaviour?

Step 7: Close the activity by referring to the objectives

Step 8: (Optional) – Get the groups' lists typed up to be issued later as a Handout

TRAINER'S NOTES

Big boys don't cry

These lists are compiled from discussions of various groups on courses run by the author. On each occasion, a Handout giving key issues was produced for participants to take away. Handouts prepared from participants' own work seem to have more validity. They have ownership of the contents, and value the aide-mémoire.

CONDITIONING

Pre-birth to Starting school

'Do you want a boy or a girl?' – son and heir syndrome.

'What colour shall we paint the nursery? What images on the wallpaper?' (there are still gender-influenced papers for sale, eg trains, Superman, or fluffy bunnies, Beatrix Potter type people/animals).

Cultural aspect – value of sons in some cultures.

Colour-coded clothes (especially those bought by older generation relatives).

Rougher handling of boy infants and toddlers.

Little boys are 'cute' when grubby; not so little girls.

Soft toys – home-making toys for girls; action toys for boys (cars, construction sets, etc).

Infants all seem to get activity centre type toys, but small boys have more toys which encourage manual dexterity, eg plastic nuts and bolts, carpentry sets, construction kits. Girls tend to get 'quieter' playthings.

Picture books and early readers tend to be sexist. Few role model books for girls (only Cinderella type, princess figures). Many books tend to portray nuclear families doing middle class things (showing Daddy mending the car; Mummy ironing; and Granny being a large old lady with hair in a 'bun', who spends the day knitting).

'Big boys don't cry'.

'Sugar and spice and all things nice', 'Slugs and snails and puppy dog tails'.

Nursery rhymes, eg Little Miss Muffet.

School to Adulthood

Girls mustn't get dirty, fight, swear or whistle (it isn't ladylike!). Girls should look nice and clean; be quietly spoken.

Boys should enjoy rough games like football and rugby. They should want to be active rather than engage in passive pursuits. 'Big boys don't cry' – or get emotional, or show that they are 'soft' in any way.

Girls shouldn't show aggression or anger. Boys are often told 'If he hits you, you hit him back.'

Girls tend to get less attention in class (because they are better behaved?). They are spoken to in negative ways whereas boys are encouraged.

Girls are expected to help in the home; many mothers still spoil sons, doing everything for them.

Girls are expected to help with younger siblings; boys get less training in parenting.

Girls are still encouraged to be 'respectable'; to 'wait for the right boy to come along'; it's acceptable for boys to 'sow wild oats'.

Adolescent girls aren't trusted to stay out late at nights; parents are more lenient with boys.

Boys can go off camping, back-packing around Europe and so on. This is not as acceptable for girls.

Girls are not encouraged to form groups; boys are encouraged to socialize in packs – rugby and football teams for example.

Boys are taught to stand up for themselves. Girls are taught to be dependent.

There are fewer female role models in the important worlds of finance, politics, and so on.

Boys can strut around wearing very little and appear macho; girls who reveal a lot of their anatomy are 'asking for trouble'.

Language and the media

There is still the he/she problem in grammar. Some authors (and legal documents) refer to 'he' throughout.

Generic terms are used to describe both genders – eg 'mankind'. It's also unfortunate that 'manager' has masculine connotations (although the root is from 'manus' – 'hand' in Latin) and 'history' (from the Greek Histor meaning wise man.)

There are more complimentary words and phrases to describe men than there are to describe women (dictionary entries). *Most* words and phrases used to describe women tend to be derogatory:

'Make an honest woman of'
'The little woman'
'The other woman'
'Woman's privilege'
'Femme fatale' (no male equivalent).

Most words and phrases used to describe men are more flattering:

'Best man'
'Handy man'
'Manly'
'Man of the world'.

Think too about the phrases 'old man' and 'old woman' and their usage; the connotations of 'bachelor' and 'spinster', of 'cook' and 'chef'; of 'master' and 'mistress'.

There is still reference to married women as eg Mrs Frank Smith, although this is becoming less frequent.

Newspapers report personal details of women, eg ' Mary Brown, a blond teenager aged 19...'; whereas they wouldn't use such descriptions for men – 'Paul Smith, a brunette aged 22 from Chigley...'

Page three girls. Male pin-ups only in specialist magazines.

Adverts and commercials tend to show the nuclear family and men and women (generally white, middle class) in stereotypical roles.

'Wife' and 'Mother-in-law' jokes (although there is an increasing number of women stand-up comics who are redressing the balance).

NATURE OR NURTURE?

This activity could usefully follow **Big boys don't cry.** It looks at how words and phrases used by adults to children and adolescents might influence their temperament and behaviour.

Objectives By the end of this activity participants will:

- have discussed the effects of 'put-downs' on children and adolescents;
- have considered any areas of self-fulfilling prophecy in their own lives which might influence present behaviour patterns.

Resources Flipchart and marker.

Time 30–45 minutes.

Method

Step 1: Trainer input to explain the activity Although it is not wise to dwell for too long on the causes of our non-assertiveness, it sometimes helps us to understand why we have developed certain patterns of behaviour. This activity looks at the phenomenon of self-fulfilling prophecy.

An example of this was an experiment performed at a school. A teacher, new to a class of pupils, was told that a certain number of the children were high achievers. These were identified to him. The children had, in fact, been chosen at random by the Head – certainly not for their ability. However, within a short time, the named children were living up to expectations and not only doing better than others in their class, but were perceived by their peers as more able and

knowledgeable. This was because of a subconscious attitude towards 'the chosen' by the teacher, with a corresponding increase in self-worth in the named pupils. It was predicted that they would do well; they became high achievers – self-fulfilling prophecy.

The system works both ways, though. More often we are told something negative about ourselves, and after a while we believe it to be true and 'live' that negativity. For example, if your parents spoke of you as 'a frail child', it is quite likely that you will grow to be a frail adult. Worse, you will *think* that you are frail, and possibly become a hypochondriac! Children told that they are clumsy may well develop into ungainly, awkward adults. Childish questions which are too often dismissed as 'stupid' may well create inhibitions to speak out in later life, and so on.

Step 2: Explain the procedure and timings Working in pairs or triads, participants will list comments which are frequently made to children and adolescents. These can be positive or negative. They should use their own experiences of childhood, perhaps their experiences as parents, or recall typical comments made by other adults to children. (10 minutes).

Step 3: Divide the group into pairs or triads. Issue notepaper and pens/pencils and set them to work Circulate, offering help if necessary to get them started.

Step 4: Reconvene the main group and draw up a composite list on the flipchart Add any ideas of your own.

Step 5: Go through the list, asking the group what repercussions the comments might have for children in later life For example, a child who is constantly referred to as 'chubby' (but still fed potato crisps and sweets) may well grow up with body-image hang-ups, or a child who is said to be 'a grafter – not clever like his sister' could develop a feeling of inferiority which lasts into adulthood, or develop alternative ways to attract or impress parents – like showing off – which could influence adult behaviour.

Step 6: Sum up, then close the activity referring to the objectives Do stress that this activity does not profess to be a great psychological study of the causes of non-assertive behaviour, but is intended to give an insight into what *might contribute to and influence* adult behaviour patterns.

Identifying and understanding a cause helps us to deal with resulting problems in a constructive manner. If participants feel that they are persistently non-assertive in some way, they may well find a cause for this in past conditioning. This self-knowledge is a valuable step towards modifying non-assertive behaviour.

STEREOTYPES

An activity which examines how society's perceptions of male and female characteristics can influence behaviour. While it is not profitable to dwell for too long on causes of non-assertive behaviour, it is often useful to understand why we might react in the way we do to certain situations. Ineffective behaviour which has been learned can, with practice, be unlearned and replaced by more assertive action.

Objectives By the end of this activity participants will:

- have considered positive and negative gender stereotypes, and discussed how these might motivate behaviour patterns;
- be more aware of how others' expectations direct our own actions.

Resources Paper, pens/pencils, flipchart and marker.

Time 1 hour.

Method

Step 1: Introduce the activity From conception – even before that sometimes – we are influenced by others' views of what we might or should be: eg 'I'm looking forward to having a son so that I can take him fishing' or 'I hope we have a granddaughter because there are such pretty little dresses I could buy her'. The offspring, in both these cases, have had their preferences pre-ordained by external influences. It has been assumed that the boy will enjoy fishing (and by implication, sports/blood sports?) and the girl will want to look pretty in frocks (concerned with her appearance; want to look 'feminine').

This activity looks at the many and various assumptions that

society makes about males and females – how each should and shouldn't behave, what attributes each should have, and so on.

Step 2: Explain the procedure and timings In small groups, participants will make lists of stereotypical qualities of boys/men and girls/women – what society expects them to be, how they are expected to behave, and 'typical' characteristics (15 minutes). Then, in the main group, lists will be compared, a composite list drawn up on the flipchart, and any issues arising will be discussed.

Step 3: Divide the group into two or three smaller sub-groups Issue paper and pens/pencils. Set groups to work. Circulate, offering suggestions to get them started if necessary (see **Trainer's notes**).

Step 4: After 15 minutes, reconvene the main group Make a composite list on flipchart paper, discussing inclusions as you go. Add any of your own if necessary.

Step 5: Sum up, then close the activity referring to the objectives.

Questions you might use:

- In what way is there a disparity between what men think about how women should be or behave and how women see themselves?
- Is there a similar disparity between how women expect men to be or behave and how men view themselves?
- Has conforming to the stereotypical feminine role served women well? Why?
- What difficulties does conforming to the typical masculine role present for men?
- How do these difficulties affect interpersonal relationships within and between the genders?

By looking at the composite list, most participants will be able to recognize elements which have influenced their development, and which might still influence behaviour. By understanding that some of these external factors affect our feelings, self-esteem, actions and reactions, we can feel less guilty about occasions where we are not assertive, and begin to unlearn unwanted behaviours.

TRAINER'S NOTES

Stereotypes

The following two lists are not exclusive, but are taken from the work of participants from several courses run by the author.

Stereotypical qualities – Women

Affectionate
Cheerful
Placid
Childlike
Compassionate
Flatterable
Gentle
Gullible
Loyal
Sensitive to others
Softly spoken
Sympathetic
Understanding
Warm
Yielding
Nurturing
Concerned with appearance
Non-user of harsh language
Eager to soothe feelings
Peacemaker
Dependable
Dependent
Excitable
Emotional
Unreliable
No good with anything mechanical/technical

Cannot cope with pressure
Cannot cope with/do not want responsibility
Home oriented
Family orientated
Puts others' needs first
Scatterbrained
Nagging
Gossipy
Unstable
Temperamental
Weak
Irrational
Lacking in confidence
Inarticulate
Maternal
Not businesslike
Won't take risks
Shy
Submissive
Easily influenced
Go to pieces in times of crisis
Modest
Live through and for others
Self-effacing
Powerless

Stereotypical qualities – Men

Brave
Strong
Dependable
Confident
Ambitious
Aggressive
Dominant
Adventurous
Macho
Defender
Concerned with self-achievement
Analytical
Willing to take a stand
Self-reliant
Childish
Forceful
Competitive
Decision maker
Self-sufficient
Individualistic
Defender of beliefs
Defender of own views
Leader
Confident
Capable
Technical
Tower of strength/protective
Stable
Athletic
Rational
Well-adjusted
Arrogant
Conceited
Provider
Self-initiated (relationships)
Vigorous
Virile
Comfortable describing own attributes/accomplishments
Powerful

Lucky you!

This activity needs a mixed group of men and women. It looks at assumptions which men and women have about each other, and how these assumptions can aid or impede assertive communication. The subject usually promotes a lively discussion!

Objectives By the end of this activity participants will:

- have discussed some of the perceived differences between the genders which create barriers to communication;
- have considered how an awareness of assumptions based on stereotypes can help assertive behaviour between genders.

Resources Flipchart paper and markers, means of attaching flipchart paper to wall.

Time 1 to 2 hours.

Method
Step 1: Explain the activity, procedure and timings This activity is about how men perceive women, and how women perceive men, both in the business world, and socially. Participants will split into two groups – all the men in one and all the women in the other. The activity is in two parts. Firstly, each group will discuss and then give a presentation on 'Why you are lucky to be you'. The women will list all the reasons why they think men are lucky to be men, and the men will discuss and list all the reasons they think women are lucky to be women. Thirty minutes will be allowed for discussion and to prepare the presentations. Each presentation should take about 5 minutes.

Step 2: Divide the group according to gender. Issue flipchart sheets and marker pens. Set groups to work Remind groups that they should consider why the opposite sex is lucky in business, social and general terms. If they need prompting, the following examples may help get them started.

Women may feel that in business, men are lucky in not having to bother too much about fashion – they are always expected to wear a suit and tie, and need not have too big a wardrobe. Some men, however, may think that women are lucky in being more able to reflect their personalities through fashion at work.

Some women may feel resentful that career breaks, because of pregnancies and child-rearing, damage their chances of achieving top jobs. Some men see these breaks as time off work – a welcome break from the 9 to 5 routine they expect to have to follow until retirement.

Step 3: Give a time check after 20 minutes to ensure that groups have started to prepare their presentations Each group will be different, some needing more, some less time to complete the task. Renegotiate times if necessary.

Step 4: Run the presentations Each presentation is likely to provoke much lively discussion with challenges, disagreements and so on. Provided this is kept light-hearted, let it run its course.

Step 5: Lead a short discussion on the findings.

Questions you might use:

- What similarities are there between the lists?
- What are the main areas of difference?
- Where are there obvious discrepancies between men's perceptions of women, and women's of themselves – and vice versa?
- In general terms, where might there be barriers to assertive communication between men and women?

Step 6: Repeat the exercise, this time asking the groups to discuss and list: (Women) – 'What annoys us about men'; and (Men) – 'What annoys us about women' Again, groups should consider the opposite sex in work, social and general terms.

Step 7: Again, allow 30 minutes for discussion and preparation, giving time checks and renegotiating times as necessary

Step 8: Run the presentations

Step 9: Lead a discussion on the issues raised by this part of the activity You could open up the discussion to include aspects of being female that women object to, and of being male that men resent. For example, why is it that in business, even if a women arranges and pays for a business lunch, invariably it is the man who is asked to try the wine and is given the bill? On business flights, why are men offered the *Financial Times* or similar to read, and women *Cosmopolitan*? Why is it assumed that men are ambitious, and prefer the business world of cut and thrust to bringing up children? Why are gentle men often seen as weak, and successful women as pushy or aggressive?

Questions you might use:

- Can you see any justification in any of the comments made about things women/men do which annoy?
- What might be done to change negative perceptions into positive ones?
- How might an awareness of how the other sex sees you help improve interpersonal relationships and communication?

Step 10: Sum up, then close the activity by referring to the objectives It is a useful exercise for both men and women to stop and consider – even, dare we suggest, ask and find out – how the other sex perceives them. An awareness and understanding of our different outlooks, attitudes and assumptions helps explain why there is often a communication barrier between men and women, especially in business.

We try to communicate on an equal footing, often carrying wrong assumptions. These differences in attitude can affect self-image and working relationships, and distort the communication process. An awareness that men and women often approach interactions from differing viewpoints is an initial step towards affecting more assertive communication.

Self-talk

We often fail to act assertively because we are afraid of possible outcomes; of what *might* happen. Thinks...'if I say that, he'll get angry/feel hurt/get upset/shout/never speak to me again...' and so on. **Self-talk** explores this barrier to assertive behaviour and suggests ways in which our own passive attitudes can be modified.

Objectives By the end of this activity participants will:

- be aware of how irrational beliefs can be a barrier to assertive behaviour;
- have identified areas of their own negative self-talk;
- have practised turning negative thoughts into rational beliefs.

Resources Notepaper, three copies of the Exercise Sheet for each participant, copy of the Handout for each participant, pens/pencils, flipchart and marker.

Time 1 to 1½ hours.

Method
Step 1: Open the activity with a short explanation of how negative self-talk can obstruct positive action Often, when faced with a potentially difficult interaction, we engage either the fight or flight response – our communication veers towards the aggressive (fight) or we avoid a confrontation by retreating (flight). This latter, passive behaviour can be the result of negative self-talk. We find all sorts of reasons why we shouldn't or couldn't face a situation; most of these reasons are unsound if looked at rationally, but nevertheless, we often

listen to, and act on, these illogical premises. If we can confront these negative thoughts and replace them with rational beliefs it will help us become more at ease with ourselves and behave more assertively.

This activity will give you the opportunity to examine areas where you typically 'go into passive mode' and to consider alternatives and possible outcomes.

Step 2: Issue a copy of the Exercise Sheet and a pen/pencil to each participant. Explain the diagram, and procedure for this step of the activity The face at the top symbolizes 'dilemma'. The 'bubbles' around the face represent the negative thoughts that flood the mind when faced with a potentially difficult exchange. The face at the bottom of the page also has bubbles surrounding it, but they represent the rational beliefs which lead to positive, assertive action.

Participants will be given a hypothetical situation, and the initial task is to insert into the top bubbles typical negative self-talk statements. For example, if the situation were about neighbours who persistently park their car in front of your house rather than on their drive, negative self-talk statements which prevent discussion of the issue could be:

'Thinks . . . it could cause bad feeling between us
. . . they might not speak to me again
. . . they might retaliate in some way
. . . they could complain about something I do'
. . . and so on.

When each bubble has a negative self-talk statement, think of positive rational counterparts to these statements and insert them into the bubbles surrounding the face at the bottom of the page.

Step 3: Write the following 'dilemma' on the flipchart

'Asking for repayment of some money you lent 6 weeks ago'

Step 4: Begin the activity Allow 10 minutes. While participants are working, reproduce the diagrams on flipchart paper with a few extra bubbles per face.

Step 5: After 10 minutes, ask for suggestions for inclusion in the bubbles on the flipchart sheet These will, of course, come from participants' own exercise sheets. If necessary, add extra bubbles to accommodate all suggestions from the group.

Step 6: Lead a short discussion on any issues arising.

Questions you might use:

- How easy was it to visualize this hypothetical situation?
- How would you feel about handling each of the counterparts – the rational thinking aspects in the bottom bubbles? What sort of assertive behaviour would each require? What follow up might be necessary?
- Would anyone like to share a similar dilemma they had to face? Do the self-talk statements bear a realistic resemblance to thoughts you experienced? What action did you eventually take? What was the outcome?

Step 3: Issue the Handout This may be useful as a reference document when working on the exercise to follow. Allow a few minutes for participants to read the handout.

Step 4: Issue further copies of the Exercise Sheet (2 for each participant). Explain the next stage in the exercise Having worked through a hypothetical situation, participants will now use the same analytical process to explore real situations where they recognize their own passive behaviour patterns.

They should first identify two situations where they fail to act (or fail to act *effectively*), because negative self-talk gets in the way. These situations could be previous communications which have failed for this reason, or ongoing issues which need to be approached more assertively. The situations may be social or work based.

Using the same principle as above, record negative self-talk statements in the top bubbles, then consider positive, rational counterparts and write these in the bubbles at the bottom of the page.

Step 5: After 10 minutes (before if several participants have completed the task) divide the group into pairs or triads. Allow a further 10–15 minutes for small group discussion of any issues arising from the exercise. Participants should be encouraged to discuss more fully the situations which have proved difficult for them, identified on the Exercise Sheets. They should challenge each others' negative self-talk where this has not been successfully countered in the bottom bubbles, and may offer constructive feedback to colleagues.

Step 6: Reconvene the main group and lead a short discussion to draw out the learning points.

Questions you might use:

- How easy/hard was it to find a rational response to an irrational thought?
- Were most negative self-talk statements irrational when analysed thoroughly?
- Does anyone still feel that negative beliefs are valid in particular situations? If so, can you give examples?

Most will be irrational, but there may well be occasions when we fail to act assertively through choice – where someone's feelings may be hurt, for example. If this choice is made based on *rational consideration* rather than on *illogical beliefs*, it is perfectly valid and justified – assertiveness is all about rational choice. However, the vast majority of situations causing stress or anxiety for us, can be dealt with if appropriate assertive behaviour is adopted.

- Was there any situation discussed in the groups where there was, or will be, only one possible outcome? How much risk was, or will be, involved? How do you feel about acting on your rational thinking?

Taking a risk is part of assertive behaviour; we have to learn to handle and live with any negative consequences.

- What are the benefits of self-talk?
- What are the disadvantages?

Step 7: Close the activity by referring to the objectives

HANDOUT

Self-talk

Questions I should ask myself:

Do I stop myself from acting assertively because I think that the only outcome would be unpleasant, unsatisfactory or harmful?

Is that rational, or are there alternative outcomes which I should consider?

Do I stop myself from acting assertively for fear I couldn't handle a response that might be disagreeable, provoking or problematic?

Is that rational? Can I think of ways I could deal with possible difficulties?

Do I stop myself from behaving assertively because I tend to take the soft option? Do I avoid exchanges which might prove to be mentally demanding or emotionally exhausting?

Is that rational?. Can I think of ways of meeting challenges?

Do I stop myself from behaving assertively because I'm afraid to take risks?

Is that rational? Yes, in some circumstances; but assertive behaviour requires risk-taking from time to time. The skill is in learning to manage the consequences of that risk-taking in an assertive manner.

EXERCISE SHEET

Self-talk

Dilemma: *State your situation here* ______________________________

____

PUT-DOWNS

An activity which helps participants recognize, and deal with, statements which are intended to patronise or demean.

Objectives By the end of this activity participants will:

- through small group work, better recognise the various forms of put-down;
- have discussed approaches to dealing with put-downs, and strategies for effectively dealing with them;
- have thought about personal situations where they have had to cope with put-downs, and practised alternative assertive responses;
- have given and received feedback on the handling of put-downs.

Resources Copy of the Exercise Sheet for each participant, pens/pencils, paper, flipchart and marker.

Time 1½ hours.

Method

Step 1: Introduce the activity Put-downs have one intention: to make the other person feel demeaned, lowered in self-esteem, inferior, or stupid. Put-downs are used in power struggles and imply, 'I know better than you', 'Your opinion is not valued', 'Your feelings and needs are not as important as mine' and so on. Put-downs violate the other person's rights.

This is not to say that put-downs are consciously used by the other person in order to hurt, demean or humiliate (although this can be the case). More often put-downs are used to demonstrate that in a one-to-

one relationship 'I am the stronger; my opinion counts'. Whether overt or covert, put-downs do wound to a greater or lesser degree. They affect confidence and self-esteem. Often they are so subtle they are difficult to recognize. Only an internal sinking feeling tells us that somehow, what has been said is in some way hurtful. We need to recognize put-downs for what they are, and learn to deal with them assertively.

Step 2: Explain the activity Working in small groups, participants will discuss various statements which are all forms of put-down. First, decide why the statement is a put-down; next suggest various possible reactions – passive, aggressive and assertive, deciding in your groups the most appropriate response to the put-down.

After discussing this group work in plenary, participants will then have the opportunity to identify personal situations where put-downs have been used, and rehearse assertive responses.

Step 3: Divide participants into small groups of 3 to 4. Issue the Exercise Sheet. Set groups to work Allow 30 minutes for groups to complete the exercise, so give a time check after about 20 minutes.

Step 4: Reconvene the main group. Discuss any issues raised by the exercise First, unpack the experience of the exercise itself.

Questions you might use:

- How easy was it to recognize that the statements were, in fact, put-downs?
- Does intonation and tone of voice play a part, or is there enough in the words used to recognize these statements for what they are?
- Do you now feel better able to recognize the subtleties of put-downs?
- Can you think of instances in your own life where put-downs have been used to effect to undervalue your judgement, to insinuate, patronize?

Next, go through each statement, taking suggestions as to the type of put-down each is. Flipchart the various examples (eg stereotyping, nagging, insinuating, questioning judgement and so on).

Go through the groups' suggested responses to the exercise statements, paying particular attention to the assertive approaches to dealing with the put-downs. Encourage participants to give constructive feedback on the suggestions.

Step 5: Ask individuals to identify one situation in their own lives where put-downs have been, or are being, used to undermine them Allow a few minutes for this (although the questioning at Step 4 should have begun this process).

Step 6: In their original groups, participants should now discuss and rehearse appropriate assertive responses to their identified put-down situations Each situation should be discussed in turn within the small groups, and the 'owner' given the opportunity to act out the situation, giving an assertive response. The usual skills practice rules should apply: the 'owner' gives an outline of the situation to other group members; one participant plays 'the other person' and group members all join in giving advice and constructive feedback. A group of 3 or 4 people will need about 30 minutes for this part of the activity.

The three aspects of dealing assertively with put-downs are:

(1) to recognize the put-down for what it is and protect your own self esteem.
(2) to let the other person know that you realize that they are trying to undermine, patronize, or manipulate you into doing or saying something you do not wish to do or say.
(3) Be short, concise and clear in your rejection of the put-down.

Step 7: Reconvene the main group to sum up The activity has shown that put-downs come in all shapes and sizes. Some are easy to identify, most are more subtle. Some are one-offs which can be dealt with quickly and relatively easily. Others may be part of a long-standing relationship where the other person is used to controlling or manipulating through the use of put-down statements.

The most important thing is being able to recognize put-downs for what they are, *and immediately*, so that the put-down behaviour can be quickly and assertively stopped.

A final point: participants should also recognize their own ability to hurt, undermine or manipulate through put-downs. Assertive behaviour means always respecting the other person's basic rights.

EXERCISE SHEET

Put-downs

Below are statements which are put-downs in various guises. First, describe what type of put-down each is, eg inferring something negative, prying, making generalizations, patronizing. In other words, what's the hidden message? There is no official jargon to learn – use your own vocabulary to describe what is intended by the person using each statement. This is to help you learn to recognize put-down statements in their various forms. Until you can immediately identify put-down statements, you will not be able to deal spontaneously with them. Next, suggest responses to each statement: one passive, one aggressive and one assertive. Obviously more thought needs to be given to how one would respond assertively to each put-down.

Example

'Are you sure you know what you are doing?' (undermining; questioning ability; questioning choice).

Passive response: 'Perhaps not, no, I'd better get help.'
Aggressive response: 'You just mind your own business and let me get on with it!'
Assertive response: 'Yes, quite sure thanks.'

Put-downs

(1) 'That's typical of a man.'
(2) 'I know it's none of my business, but...'
(3) 'Don't you worry about that; I'll deal with Paul.'
(4) '*You* don't need assertiveness training!'

(5) 'You're not one of those feminists are you?'
(6) 'Good grief! Haven't you finished that yet?'
(7) 'If I were you, I would . . .'
(8) 'I know Jane well – you're surely not suggesting she'd do that?'
(9) 'Well we all know why *she* got promotion!'
(10) 'You must go back straight away and tell him that . . .'
(11) 'If you would only co-operate occasionally, we wouldn't have these rows.'
(12) 'Of course, you've always been shy, haven't you?'
(13) 'The trouble is, you always get too involved.'
(14) 'I know you have difficulty with mechanical things, so I've written out easy instructions for you to follow.'
(15) 'You're so stuck in your ways!'
(16) 'You're not busy on Thursday are you?'
(17) 'We all know your views on that.'
(18) 'Honestly, how can you believe that!'
(19) 'Go on, cry – that's a typical woman's reaction.'
(20) 'We must do something about that temper of yours!'

Behaviour review

No one likes being criticized, and most of us find it difficult to give criticism. However, relationships can actually benefit if things we do which hurt, upset, offend or harm are pointed out in a skilful, positive, assertive way. At work, too, it is far better for an individual to be given the opportunity to improve behaviour or attitude, or change the way they do things. This can only be done by exchange of information – giving and receiving constructive criticism.

This activity takes a thorough look at the subject of feedback. It suggests techniques for giving and receiving constructive feedback in a skilled and sensitive way. The activity should be preceded by trainer input on handling criticism to include areas such as Negative Assertion, Negative Enquiry and Fogging, and the difference between constructive criticism and destructive put-down behaviour. Information on all these elements is included in most textbooks on assertiveness training.

Objectives By the end of this activity participants will:

- recognize the risks involved in giving criticism, and be aware of ways of minimizing these risks;
- have discussed the implications of not giving criticism where it is warranted;
- be aware of the advantages of asking for feedback on behaviour, performance, etc;
- have practised giving and receiving feedback.

Resources Copy of the Handout for each participant, flipchart and marker, means of attaching flipchart sheets to the wall.

Time 2 hours.

Method

Step 1: Introduce the activity Most people find giving or receiving criticism a stressful experience. Fear of criticism inhibits assertive behaviour. The very word 'criticism' has negative connotations of confrontation, censure, disapproval and hurt feeling; yet feedback – to give it another name – whether positive or negative, can be important and useful. It gives us another's opinion of how we are functioning, how we are performing in our job, of behaviour which might be improved, and so on. It is a way of learning more about ourselves and the effect our behaviour has on others. Constructive feedback can increase our self-awareness, offer options which we are free to accept or reject, and encourage learning. Rather than avoid criticism, we should, perhaps, learn to consider feedback as a right which we can request from others in order to improve and develop relationships at home, in our social lives and at work. This activity looks at ways of offering and receiving feedback which leave both parties feeling good about themselves.

Step 2: Using a flipchart, list advantages of asking for feedback from others Use the brainstorming technique, ie list every contribution, without comment, however obscure the suggestion may appear. Advantages can derive from work, social or home situations and could include things like:

- to increase self-awareness
- to be given ideas on how to improve effectiveness
- to have another's opinion of strengths
- to have another's opinion of weaknesses
- to be reassured that what I am doing is correct
- to assess areas for improvement
- to see if I see myself as others see me
- to explore other ways of behaving
- to consider whether there is anything about my attitude which could be improved
- to reassess the image I present.

Attach flipchart sheet to the wall where everyone can see it.

Step 3: Remind participants of techniques for asking for constructive feedback Negative Enquiry is where you actively search out criticism

of behaviour, attitude, performance, image, etc, for the purpose of self-improvement. For example, if you fail an interview and ask for constructive criticism, you may well be given information on which you can work to improve performance in future interview situations.

Step 4: Go through the list asking for suggestions how Negative Enquiry might be applied in each case

Step 5: On another sheet of flipchart paper, brainstorm reasons which prevent us from asking for criticism These could include:

– I couldn't handle sarcasm, or being patronized
– they may criticize something I can do nothing about
– I'll feel bad about myself
– I'll feel bad about the other person
– I get hurt easily
– even if unfair, I'll take the criticism to heart
– I'm not confident enough
– I'll react aggressively
– I'll counter-attack
– I don't want to hear anything negative about myself.

Attach flipchart sheet to the wall.

Step 6: Again, go through the list asking for comment and ways of overcoming the difficulties described

Step 7: Brainstorm and record the risks involved in giving criticism and negative feedback Ask participants why they might hesitate in giving criticism. Reasons could include:

– it will cause me great stress
– I will feel bad about myself telling them something which they don't want to hear
– it could damage our relationship
– they may no longer like me
– more politic to keep quiet
– it may end up in a slanging match
– they may get angry
– they may be indignant
– they may be hurt
– they may get upset
– I may not be able to cope with their emotions

- they may emphatically disagree
- they may misunderstand what I am trying to say
- they may become even more stubborn
- they may distort my words to suit their own ends
- it might risk the relationship while still having no effect on their behaviour.

Step 8: Using the list above, discuss the implications of not giving negative feedback Reasons could include:

- the other person loses an opportunity to learn and develop
- barriers could develop; the relationship might suffer if feedback is not given
- at best, the status quo will be maintained; at worst, the problem may grow, in the mind, out of all proportion
- there is an increasing chance that a small issue will eventually become a confrontation
- if there is no criticism, there is very little chance of there being any change
- the other person may continue to be unaware that there is anything wrong with behaviour, image, performance, etc.

Step 9: Issue and go through the Handout Ensure that each stage of the activity so far, and the contents of the Handout, are clear in the minds of participants, because the final part of the activity will be a skills practice in giving and receiving criticism.

Step 10: Explain procedure for the next part of the activity Participants will work in pairs (one triad if there is an odd number). Each person will in turn ask their partner for feedback on their performance as a member of the assertiveness training course. Their partner will give constructive feedback which should include positive and negative elements. The recipient of the feedback can then practise receiving that criticism in the most appropriate way – by accepting the criticism (Negative Assertion with more Negative Enquiry follow-up?); disagreeing with the criticism (criticism which is basically untrue, or too broadly based, or person-orientated rather than a criticism of behaviour, for example); or Fogging.

If the criticism is realistic, justified and accepted, participants should make sure they do not apologise, get defensive or angry, or put themselves down. They should receive any criticism with direct eye contact, firm tone of voice and appropriate body language which

conveys to the other person, 'I'm OK; I can occasionally make mistakes; neither I nor anyone else is perfect.'

Step 11: Divide the group into pairs. Set the pairs to work Circulate, offering advice and constructive criticism to pairs, ensuring that the feedback offered by partners is clear, direct and useful. The timings for this part of the activity will vary from group to group, but about 15 minutes should be enough for the skills practice and for partners to discuss what they learned about giving and receiving criticism.

Step 12: Reconvene the main group. Lead a brief discussion on the activity Ask participants to identify the key learning points. The discussion should concentrate on the practical aspects of giving and receiving criticism, and positive recommendations for more assertive communication.

Step 13: Close the activity by referring to the objectives

HANDOUT

Behaviour review

The following tips are just that – some suggestions on asking for, giving and receiving criticism. Different situations with different people will call for different approaches. You don't have to follow every guideline every time!

Asking for feedback – Negative Enquiry

Who? Actively invite criticism only from people you trust, and whose opinion you respect.

When? You can initiate communication by asking for constructive feedback – after an unsuccessful interview for example – or you can ask for more detail through Negative Enquiry after receiving realistic criticism, eg 'Yes, I accept that I didn't handle that very assertively; in what ways do you think I could improve?' (In fact, this is using Negative Assertion and Negative Enquiry together – quite a powerful combination.) Choose your moment wisely so that the other person has time to give a considered and constructive response.

How? By taking your courage in both hands and practising all your assertion skills, recognizing that by taking the initiative and encouraging negative as well as positive feedback, you are more likely to generate respect in the other person than disrespect for not being perfect!

Why? It opens the way for honest communication; gives ideas on how to improve performance; gives a different perspective of behaviour or image; improves relationships – and remember, you don't have to accept the criticism. Listen well and assess for yourself the other person's views.

Receiving criticism

Listen and acknowledge Listen to what is being said, not what you think is being implied. Weigh up the criticism. Is it valid, invalid or a put-down? Whichever, acknowledge that you have heard and understood either by a simple 'OK' or 'Right'. This isn't saying that the other person *is* right, and that you are agreeing with them – just that you have heard and are willing to communicate. An alternative is to repeat what they said back to them in question form, eg 'Are you saying that you think I should be more assertive with John?' This not only tells the other person that you are prepared to listen, but gives you time to consider the criticism and your response more fully.

Define the criticism Deal with put-downs quickly if you can, leaving the critic in no doubt that you recognize the hidden message. Try not to cap one put-down with another. Clever though this might be, (and however good you feel about yourself initially) it is basically aggressive behaviour. If you don't recognize a put-down for what it is at the time it occurs – and we often think afterwards 'Hang on! that was a snide remark when she said...' – you can always confront the critic later at an appropriate time.

If the criticism is valid, admit graciously using the words of the critic, eg 'Yes, I was hasty when I said...' or 'Yes, I did forget to lock the back door last night'. Don't get defensive: 'I was so tired last night that...'. Don't counter-attack: 'Well, you were the last up; why didn't you lock it?' or over-apologize 'I'm so sorry – I'm getting so forgetful – I really am sorry about that'.

If the criticism is invalid, look the other person in the eye and state your case clearly and with conviction, making sure that content and delivery match, eg 'That's just not true; I'm not a vindictive person'. This can be followed by a statement of self-affirmation, 'I spent a lot of time explaining the situation to Sally; I was pleased with the way I handled it.'

If the criticism is too broadly based but has an element of validity, acknowledge and deal with those elements which are realistic, but separate yourself from broad negative evaluations, eg 'You're always late'; 'Today I *am* late for work – I'm sorry. However, this is an exception; I'm usually in the office by nine.'

If the criticism doesn't worry you too much, Fogging is a way of calmly acknowledging that there *may* be some truth in what is being said, eg 'You may have a point', 'You're probably right'. Neither agree, nor disagree with the critic. Merely acknowledge the criticism, then move on.

Giving feedback

Set up rapport Don't burst forth with the criticism. Have some conversation first.

Positive with negative Most people respond to praise, recognition and encouragement. If you can preface negative feedback with something positive about the person or relationship, the negative statement is more likely to be favourably received. Do not wrack your brains for positive comments however – the praise has to be genuine, eg 'I'm really happy with the way you've settled in here; the patients are responding well to you. I do feel, though, that you need to take more care with your paperwork.'

Distasteful/embarrassing criticism Criticism of someone's personal habits or hygiene is very awkward to deal with. Consider the points above. Be specific and direct with the negative feedback, while being sensitive to the other person's feelings. Sandwich the negative feedback. Say something positive – give the criticism in a kind but direct way – change the subject so that you both leave the conversation on a friendly note.

Be specific Avoid generalizations and general comments such as 'You didn't handle that very well'. Tell the person what it was they did which was ineffective. Try to comment on observable behaviour. Avoid criticizing something a person can do nothing about, on their apparent motives or shortcomings. Direct feedback only toward behaviour that an individual can do something about.

Give details Detailed feedback gives more opportunity for learning, eg 'You handled that well because you really listened to the client's needs, and gave him the opportunity to explain . . .'.

Empathise It sometimes helps to let the other person know that you can see their point of view, eg 'I realize that what I am going to say may disappoint you, but I can't put you forward for promotion because . . .'.

Keep calm Don't let the other person see that you are anxious about giving feedback. Use relaxation techniques; keep the voice steady and even; remember eye contact and body language; don't allow yourself to get angry or intimidated.

Keep to the point Don't allow yourself to get side-tracked. Don't bring up issues irrelevant to the point under discussion.

Allow the other person space Everyone has the right to accept or reject feedback; the right to be the judge of their own behaviour and to defend that right. Whether or not your feedback is acted upon is a matter for their decision.

Don't demand change You cannot impose beliefs, opinions or attitudes on others. At best, demands for change are met with initial resistance: at worst, intransigence and feelings of resentment. Skilful, constructive feedback offers people information about themselves from which they can learn and act upon if desired.

Use 'I' statements Take ownership of the feedback. Avoid 'You are...' type statements as these suggest unanimous agreement about a person's behaviour or attitudes. Open with 'I think...' or 'In my view...' or 'I feel that...'

Focus on behaviour Criticise behaviour, not the person, eg 'I was hurt when you said...' not 'You are insensitive'.

Understanding Check that the other person has understood you correctly.

Stereotypes Avoid statements such as 'I would expect that of a woman' or 'You're behaving like a spoilt brat!'

Change Be aware that things may not change as a result of the feedback. Be equally aware that things may change. However skilfully you offer criticism, there is always the chance that the other person will be hurt or annoyed, and that your relationship might change as a result. You need to weigh the pros and cons of *not* offering negative feedback. Similarly, the recipient of the criticism needs to consider the consequences of not acting on negative feedback.

I CAN HANDLE IT

This activity offers participants skills practice in receiving criticism. It should be preceded by full trainer input on handling positive and negative feedback including how to cope with justified and unjustified criticism, put-downs, criticism based on value judgements, criticism which is too broad based, and areas such as Negative Assertion, Self-Affirmation, Negative Enquiry and Fogging. It could usefully follow the activity **Behaviour review.**

Objectives By the end of this activity participants will:

- have identified criticisms which have been levelled at them in the past, both valid and invalid;
- have replayed situations where criticism has been given, using various assertive techniques for handling criticism;
- have offered constructive feedback to colleagues on ways to improve their response to different types of criticism.

Resources Sheets of paper and pen/pencil for each participant, container (hat or box) in which to put lists, (*optional*) – copy of Handout from activity **Behaviour review** for each participant.

Time Dependent on the number of participants in the group

Method

Step 1: Explain the activity Initially, participants will work alone to make two lists of criticisms – one of justified criticisms which could be levelled at them, and which they know to have some validity; the second, criticisms which are untrue or too broadly based, put-downs,

or labels which just don't apply and which would need to be challenged.

These lists will then be exchanged with those of colleagues. Participants will take it in turn to level a criticism at another group member who will handle that criticism appropriately. The rest of the group and the trainer will then offer constructive feedback to those practising the giving and receiving of criticism.

Step 2: Arrange chairs in a circle or horseshoe shape in readiness for the skills practice. Issue paper and pen/pencil to each participant. Begin the exercise Instruct participants to write their name at the top of the sheet, then to list the valid criticisms – four or five if they can. They should draw a line across the page to distinguish valid from invalid criticisms, and then list several unjustified criticisms, put-downs, criticisms which are too broadly based, aggressive criticisms, etc. Participants should draw on social, home and work situations for examples. 15 minutes will be allowed.

Step 3: When each participant has listed several examples of valid and invalid criticisms, instruct them to fold their paper and put it into the container Go around the group collecting the lists. Mix them up well in the container.

Step 4: Pass the container around the group. Each participant should take out one folded sheet If, by chance, they draw their own list, this should be returned to the container and another taken out.

Step 5: Allow a few minutes for participants to read the lists and to decide which criticism they are going to direct to the 'owner' of the list they have drawn They should choose just one either valid or invalid criticism. If a justified criticism is chosen, constructive criticism techniques can be practised. If a put-down, or accusatory criticism is to be practised, participants should decide how to phrase the criticism realistically.

Step 6: Decide on one person to begin the activity. They should name the person whose list they have drawn and direct one of the criticisms listed at them. The 'owner' will respond appropriately Other group members should be encouraged to give constructive feedback to the person receiving the criticism. Add any comments of your own. Things to look out for are:

- eye contact
- body language
- appropriate phrasing
- tone of voice
- tendency to over-react
- tendency to become defensive
- tendency to apologize/retreat
- Negative Assertion (where appropriate)
- Negative Enquiry (where appropriate)
- Self-Affirmation (where appropriate).

Step 7: Continue the exercise until everyone has given and received criticism. If time allows, give participants the opportunity to respond to one more example of negative feedback If you intend to run the exercise a second time, ask participants to cross off the criticism already practised from the list from which they've been working and to pass the sheets to the right. Everyone now has a new list to work from. Repeat Steps 5 and 6, asking participants to choose a criticism from a different area, ie if a valid criticism was practised last time, choose a put-down or unjustified criticism this time.

Step 8: Process the activity.

Questions you might use:

- How did it feel criticizing another person?
- Was it easier to accept criticism or to give it?
- How easy was it to invite more criticism through Negative Enquiry?
- If you disagreed with the criticism, was it easy or difficult to self-affirm after disagreeing? Why?
- Was it easier to accept valid criticism or disagree with invalid? Why?
- Why do people find it so hard to handle criticism?
- What is the most useful or important aspect you have learned about assertively handling criticism?

Step 8: Sum up Criticism is difficult to take for a number of reasons. We have all been conditioned through childhood experiences; we have all been labelled at some stage for being stupid, lazy, slapdash, clumsy, or for being typically a woman ... or a man ... or a Pisces or Taurus! We must all have suffered from criticisms where we have

been denigrated as people rather than an aspect of our behaviour discussed. Most of us like to be liked or approved of by everyone, and some of us feel that to make mistakes, or not to be perfect at all times, is tantamount to interpersonal failure. It is hardly surprising that criticism is so difficult to cope with.

However, by learning to recognize the type of criticism which is being delivered, and to deal with each situation with appropriate assertive responses, as practised here, confidence and self-esteem will grow. You will not avoid or be apprehensive about giving or receiving criticism, because you have various coping techniques at your fingertips. You will be well prepared for it, and will know that, handled skilfully, constructive feedback can be useful to both giver and receiver.

Step 9:* (Optional) *– If this activity has not been preceded by 'Behaviour review', issue the Handout from that activity This Handout gives suggestions on asking for, giving and receiving feedback.

Step 10: Close the activity

CHAPTER 5

REQUESTS AND REFUSALS

RIGHTS

This activity looks at an issue central to assertiveness: respecting your own and others' basic rights.

Objectives By the end of this activity participants will:

- have reached a group consensus on a list of basic rights;
- have the means to compile a personal list of rights (if different from above);
- better understand the assertive belief that we all have personal rights;
- have considered how they have allowed themselves or others to violate personal rights;
- be better equipped to think positively about themselves;
- be more aware that the recognition of rights is a two-way process.

Resources Copy of the Handout for each participant, copy of **Trainer's notes**, flipchart and marker, (*optional*) – typewriter/typist and photocopier.

Time 1½ hours.

Method

Step 1: Introduce the activity One of the central tenets of assertive philosophy is the belief that we all have personal rights. Acting assertively on these rights (rather than demanding or repressing) helps us to see ourselves in a more positive way. Confidence and self-esteem grows. This in turn affects relationships and how we interact with the outside world in general. It cannot be stressed enough that *everyone* has basic human rights. Some training courses concentrate on personal rights without giving enough attention to the rights of others too. Assertiveness is not about one-upmanship or getting one's own way; it's not about demanding, or even having requests granted – the other person has as much right to refuse as you have to ask. An assertive person will always consider whether they are treating the other person with as much respect as they, themselves, would like to receive.

Although there are some basic human rights which appear in all literature on assertiveness, there are almost as many variations on the theme as there are books on the subject. Rather than impose just one 'Bill of Rights', this activity offers an extensive list of rights, compiled from the views of several authors. From this list, participants, as a group, can select, amend, adapt or add until they are satisfied with a set of personal rights from which they can work with confidence.

Step 2: Explain the procedure for the activity Participants will each be given a list of personal rights. This has been compiled in order to give as extensive a choice as possible. There may well still be omissions, however. The task of the group is to consider this list and from it draw up a 'Bill of Rights' which participants will be happy to work from for the duration of the course. As it is unlikely that there will be complete agreement, individuals should feel free to amend or adapt the final group list in order to compile a personal 'Bill of Rights' with which they feel confident.

Step 3: Issue copies of the Handout Allow participants a few minutes to read through the list.

Step 4: Taking each point in turn, discuss and decide whether it should be included in the group list. Flipchart agreed rights The pros and cons of the concept itself and the wording of the right should be considered, as should the implications in implementing that right.

It may be necessary for you to ask the group to prioritize, and restrict the list to 10 or 12 rights.

Step 5: Divide participants into small groups of 3 or 4 people Instruct groups to discuss which of the rights on the agreed list they find difficult to implement. Ask them to give examples of present behaviour which allows self or others to violate or restrict these rights.

Step 6: (Optional) – While small group discussions are taking place, type up and photocopy the group's agreed Bill of Rights

Step 7: Reconvene the main group for brief discussion and summing up Ask for observations from the small group discussions; field any questions.

Rather than adopt a tailor-made Bill of Rights, it is preferable that individuals adopt rights which are appropriate for both themselves and other people with whom they have contact. This is why it is important to construct your own Bill of Rights – ones which have meaning for you and which you can apply to your own life. It is also important not to duck issues, just because a particular right is difficult to achieve. For example, the right to make your own decisions and live with the consequences may be difficult for someone who has spent a lifetime being dependent, but this doesn't mean it's a right to be neglected.

Step 8: (Optional) – Issue the group's Bill of Rights. Close the activity by referring to the objectives

HANDOUT

Rights

This extensive list of rights is compiled from the writings of several authors on assertiveness. This activity suggests that, rather than working to an imposed list, it is preferable for individuals to construct their own 'Bill of Rights' which has personal meaning and relevance.

Everyone's rights

(1) To be treated as an equal, regardless of gender, race, age or disability.
(2) To be treated with respect as a capable human being.
(3) To decide how to spend my time.
(4) To ask for what I want.
(5) To ask for feedback on things such as my performance, behaviour, image.
(6) To be listened to and taken seriously.
(7) To have an opinion.
(8) To hold political beliefs.
(9) To cry.
(10) To make mistakes.
(11) To say 'No' without feeling guilty.
(12) To state my needs.
(13) To set my own priorities.
(14) To express my feelings.
(15) To say 'Yes' for myself without feeling selfish.
(16) To change my mind.
(17) To fail occasionally.
(18) To say 'I don't understand'.

(19) To make statements which have no logical basis and which I do not have to justify.
(20) To ask for information.
(21) To be successful.
(22) To express my beliefs.
(23) To adhere to my own set of values.
(24) To take time to make decisions.
(25) To take responsibility for my own decisions.
(26) To have privacy.
(27) To admit 'I don't know.'
(28) To change/develop as a human being.
(29) To choose whether or not to get involved in another person's problems.
(30) To decline to be responsible for someone else's problems.
(31) To look after my own needs.
(32) To have time and space to be alone.
(33) To be an individual.
(34) To ask for information from professionals.
(35) Not to be dependent on others' approval.
(36) To be the judge of my own worth.
(37) To choose how to behave/respond in a given situation.
(38) To be independent.
(39) To be me; not the person others want me to be.
(40) Not to assert myself.

TRAINER'S NOTES

Rights

The following suggestions may help start discussion of the rights listed in the Handout. Only the first 10 statements are covered here, but this should give some indication of the type of issues which could be raised.

(1) As with most of the rights, most people have little difficulty in accepting them for others, but it is often difficult to consider, or treat, *ourselves* as equal. Consider words like 'disability' here. Would the word 'ability' carry the same meaning? Are some people 'more equal than others'? Is treating people as equals the same as treating all people the same?

(2) Again, we do not always treat *ourselves* with respect. Even if you believe you have this right, it doesn't mean that you'll always *be* treated with respect; but if you believe it, you will approach situations differently, your body language will give a positive message, and you will be more likely to gain respect of others.

Does *everyone* deserve to be treated with respect?

Does respect have to be earned?

(3) Often, we are so occupied with pandering to the needs and demands of others, that our own wishes and needs are suppressed. For example – going to the theatre or cinema because your partner wants to go, when you would prefer to spend your time in another way; or sharing a sea, sun and sand holiday when you would prefer a city cultural break.

Do men always have to be ambitious, seeking promotion, spending their working days fighting to get ahead? Might they want to spend their time in another way – sharing child-rearing for example? Should

women spend their time at home bringing up the children? Should they pursue self-development and careers? These are all questions related to deciding what to do with personal time.

(4) To ask, yes; not demand. The other person also has rights – to refuse your request being one. What are the implications of not asking for what you want? What are the risks involved in making direct requests? What happens to self-esteem when, rather than asking directly, you continually *hope* someone may *guess* what you want, or when you go along with what other people want rather than express your own needs?

(5) What are the advantages of asking for constructive feedback. What are the risks?

(6) Remember that rights go both ways. You will also have to be a good listener. What can you do if people do not listen to you? What can you do if your views are seldom considered important or relevant?

(7) Not just *have* opinions, but the right to voice them even when they go against the majority view. If you believe strongly in a cause, you don't have to justify that opinion to others, apologize for your views, or get drawn into arguments which challenge your opinion or belief.

(8) Again, you do not have to justify or explain religious or political beliefs, but you do have the right to express beliefs should you wish to do so.

(9) Why do we feel it inappropriate to cry publicly? Is it OK for men to cry? Why do we feel embarrassed, or that we've failed ourselves in some way if we cry?

(10) Nobody's perfect. We all make mistakes from time to time. We are human and fallible. So why are we so guilt-ridden, ashamed or defensive when the occasional mistake occurs? Why do we believe that making a mistake is unacceptable or a sign of stupidity? Far better to learn by mistakes; support and encourage self and others when mistakes occur, and recognize that a mistake doesn't mean that you are intrinsically witless or behaviourally unsound!

Broken record

This activity needs to be preceded by detailed trainer input on the Broken Record technique – verbatim repetitions; changed phraseology without a change of meaning; matching content, delivery and body language; empathy; workable compromise, etc. In addition, various applications of the technique will need to be addressed. Most textbooks on assertiveness will fully cover this.

The activity requires the trainer to act the part of 'the other person' in each instance, and to relentlessly pursue a goal so that the participant practising Broken Record is thoroughly tested in the technique.

Objectives By the end of this activity participants will:

- each have confronted (and hopefully, withstood) a persistent interlocutor;
- have practised either refusing a request, asserting their rights, or maintaining a point of view in the face of persuasive or diverting arguments.

Resources Copy of **Trainer's notes**.

Time Approximately 5 minutes for each participant.

Method

Step 1: Introduce the activity Anyone who watches television interviews with politicians will have seen Broken Record in action. However persistent, persuasive or abusive the interviewer becomes, if the politician doesn't want to answer the question, she or he will merely repeat what they want the listening public to hear, over and

over again, sometimes altering the phraseology, but basically saying the same thing until the interviewer gives up and moves onto another topic.

The following is a paraphrase of just such an interview:

Interviewer:	You say that you would not put up taxes.
Politician:	I'm saying that there are ways of raising money other than by direct taxation.
Interviewer:	But these other methods take time to reap benefits. Initially, to fund your programme, surely tax rises are inevitable?
Politician:	There are other ways of raising money which would be preferable to raising taxes.
Interviewer:	Well what are these methods – I'm sure we'd all love to hear about them!
Politician:	There are many ways. I'm not going to hypothesize at this stage because we don't know what the economic climate will be, but there are ways of raising money other than by direct taxation.
Interviewer:	But what if...
Politician:	I'm not going to hypothesize...
Interviewer:	OK. It's obvious to me that you don't have any real answers on taxation, so let's press on.

The technique can be used to refuse a request – say 'No' – or to refuse to be drawn into talking about an issue (as above). It can also be used to good effect in asserting your rights. For example, if you want a job of work corrected, and the individual concerned offers all manner of excuses and reasons why this can't be done, you can persist in your request/demand using this technique. There may be times when an individual tries to put you down, or challenges your opinion, or attacks a cause you hold dear. Again, Broken Record can be used to good effect when you want to hold firm.

People practised in assertion will find, after a while, that Broken Record becomes a skill which can be used to great effect in all manner of situations. When two people skilled in the technique have a head-to-head, it will soon become obvious to both that there is no point in banging your head against a brick wall. Assertive people respect assertive behaviour when they meet it and will be ready to either change the topic (as in the above example) or negotiate a win/win situation.

Step 2: Explain the activity Sometimes you are aware, in advance, of a situation which will require the Broken Record technique. Often, however, out of the blue someone will make a request which is difficult to refuse, or you may find an articulate, persuasive salesperson on your doorstep, or you suddenly get resistance to a request from an unsuspected source.

This activity will test participants' ability to spontaneously apply the Broken Record technique.

You (the trainer) will be 'the other person' in each instance, and will test each participant on their skills. Choosing individuals at random, you will 'be' the difficult salesperson or the awkward subordinate. Participants will use their assertive skills, making sure that content, delivery and body language match, to withstand the 'onslaught'. They should remember that negotiation and/or workable compromise are ultimate options.

Step 3: Begin the activity Identify one participant; choose a topic on which to test them (see **Trainer's notes**). Be as persuasive, argumentative – even abusive – as you think necessary to test their skills. Don't let them off the hook too easily.

Step 4: At the end of each interaction, ask for observations and constructive feedback from the rest of the group Add any comments of your own from the perspective of 'the other person' and as trainer.

Step 5: Continue until each participant has had at least one opportunity to practise their skills Ensure that every individual has had a positive experience of Broken Record.

Step 6: Sum up, then close the activity referring to the objectives As with any skills practice, it is beneficial to rehearse real-life situations. However, the unexpected does happen, and often we are suddenly presented with a situation where we need to assert – and reassert – ourselves to get our views across, or our needs and feelings recognized. This activity simulated such occurrences, and had the benefit of being a rehearsal with feedback from supportive colleagues.

TRAINER'S NOTES

Broken record

You will need to practise how to harass, badger, persuade, wheedle, tempt, threaten, convince and so on before attempting this activity. The analogy of the interviewer/politician used in the activity is a useful one. If you need guidance, watch one or two television interviews for ideas.

Choose a different participant at random. Explain the scenario if necessary, or launch straight into a dialogue. Choose your own scenarios appropriate to your group. Alternatively, there follow some topic suggestions.

(1) Ask the participant if they have a cause about which they feel strongly. Their task is to avoid discussion of the issue with you. Yours is to try and goad them into a debate on the subject.

Alternatively, begin a discussion on their favoured cause, then challenge one aspect of their views. Their task is to hold their ground.

(2) You are the boss. You want the participant to agree to attend a 4-day conference at a residential centre some 200 miles away. The participant has home commitments which take priority over business away from home. The participant should make her/his priorities known, and refuse.

(3) You work for an employment agency which is able to offer £10 per hour (the going rate) for the work applied for by the participant. Your controlling committee want to cut costs. You get commission if you can secure the position for much less. However, you want this participant for this post. The participant (who knows the going rates) should initiate a conversation to assert her/his rights to the full £10.

(4) You are in charge of a car bodywork shop. The participant has required you to repair some accident damage to the front wing. The dent is still visible – not adequately hammered out, and the respray is a slightly lighter blue than the rest of the car's paintwork. You want payment; the participant needs the job redone.

(5) You have made a remark which the participant finds offensive. They require an apology of you. You should goad them further, tease them, be dismissive, joke with them – anything rather than offer the required retraction and apology.

(6) You have been told by your company that although there is a money back guarantee on faulty goods, you should do everything possible to avoid this action. The participant has only her/his lunch hour to return faulty goods to your store. She/he wants a refund so that a similar item can be purchased elsewhere.

(7) You are on an interview panel and ask a question which the participant finds impertinent or irrelevant. You should badger away at the point. The participant should make it clear that she/he is not prepared to answer that question.

(8) You are a teacher. The participant is a parent whose child has been bullied. They want to know what, specifically, is going to be done about the situation. The participant should persist in her/his right to know what action is to be taken. You should continue to be vague for as long as possible.

(9) The participant needs to know more detail about their proposed treatment. You, as their GP, feel they needn't know particulars about their condition or medication.

(10) The participant has lent you an electric drill and wants it returned. You have, in turn, lent it to someone else without getting prior consent from the participant. The participant wants the drill returned at once. You make every possible excuse rather than own up to the fact that you no longer have it.

Skills practice – refusing a request

Identify a participant and just begin a dialogue without prior briefing.

'Could you look after my dog this weekend?'

'Could I interest you in one of these prints – painted by people with severe disabilities.'

'Would you bring coffee for Mr Bridges and myself please?'

'Would you like to come to dinner with Margaret and Bob?'

'I'd like you to work overtime tonight to get these reports ready for committee tomorrow.'

I WOULD IF I COULD, BUT . . .

When refusing requests many people find it difficult to give a direct 'No'. One of the usual responses is 'I would if I could, but I can't because...' This activity looks at the possible repercussions of offering excuses, and allows participants to practise ways of refusing requests which are both assertive and conclusive, and with which individuals feel comfortable.

This activity should be preceded by general trainer input on how to say 'No' (**Broken Record** technique, **Negative Assertion** and so on). It could usefully be followed by the skills practice activity, **No excuses**.

Objectives By the end of this activity participants will:

- have practised refusing requests in a manner acceptable to them;
- have received feedback on the effectiveness of their assertiveness;
- have had the opportunity to observe, and offer advice to, colleagues on their ability to refuse requests in an assertive way.

Resources One copy of the Exercise Sheet for each participant, flipchart and marker, (*optional*) – Handout.

Time 1 hour.

Method

Step 1: Explain the activity Participants will work in groups of three, practising refusing requests so that (*a*) the other person realizes that 'No' means just that, and (*b*) everyone is comfortable with the measure of empathy shown, and the amount of explanation for the refusal. Each participant will take turns to make a request, refuse a request, and observe and give feedback.

Step 2: Trainer input on the pitfalls of offering excuses (See **Trainer's notes**.) Write up the stages of the three-point plan on a flipchart.

Step 3: Divide the group into triads If there is an odd number, have one group of four, two of whom will act as observers at each practice.

Step 4: Issue Exercise Sheets. Explain procedure and timings Give participants a few moments to read the instructions.

Explain that participants will take turns to make a request of one of their group. That person should refuse the request adopting the three-point plan, using words with which they feel comfortable. Observers should assess effectiveness against the listed criteria, and offer feedback after each practice. The person refusing the request may continue to practise, using the advice of colleagues, until they feel confident with their response. Each person must have at least one turn at each role: requester, refuser and observer. 15–30 minutes to complete the exercise.

Step 5: Begin the activity Circulate around groups to offer advice if necessary.

Step 6: Reconvene the main group for brief discussion Ask for observations. Take questions.

Step 7: Sum up, issue the Handout (optional) then close the activity Delivering a stark 'No' to a request can provoke all manner of reactions in the other person. If delivered as an abrupt word of warning to a child about to put his fingers into a light socket, for example, it may startle the child, but the shock is minor to the one he might otherwise have suffered! That is an acceptable use of the single word 'No'. Explanations can follow later.

In other circumstances, just saying 'No' can raise hackles, or make the other person feel rejected or resentful. This is why most of us feel more comfortable offering some kind of explanation to soften the blow of a direct refusal. However, it is important to keep reasons short and to the point, and to include the word 'No' in any refusal so that it leaves the other person in no doubt as to our firmness of intent.

EXERCISE SHEET

I would if I could, but...

Requesters
Choose from one of the following, or make up a request of your own.

'I've got a few days' leave to take. Will it be OK if I come and stay with you next weekend?'

'We've been invited to a wedding in July. We can't very well take the dog as it's a long journey, then there's the wedding itself and the reception, and it will be too hot in July to leave him in the car all that time. Would you look after him for me?'

'I'm organizing a summer fair in aid of charity. Could you run one of the stalls?'

'Martin's standing down this year; can I nominate you for the post of Treasurer?'

'Can I borrow your portable typewriter please?'

'I know I'm always asking favours of you, but could we change shifts next week?'

Refusers
For the purpose of this exercise, you are to refuse any request made of you. Remember to use the word 'No' quite firmly somewhere in your refusal, but moderate your response, in your own way, so that the other person does not feel rejected or resentful.

Remember body language, tone and pitch of voice and so on.

Content and approach must match.

Observers

Check that the word 'No' is actually used, not just implied.

Watch for facial expression and body language.

Has enough information been given to back up the refusal?

Was too much given by way of explanation?

How relaxed and secure did the refuser seem?

TRAINER'S NOTES/HANDOUT

I would if I could, but...

It is perfectly acceptable to moderate a refusal by saying something like, 'I understand your difficulty, and am really sorry that I can't help...', but it is also important to actually state 'No' somewhere in your refusal, to make it absolutely clear that you won't be shifted from your position; eg 'I would help out if I could, but I've a prior commitment on Wednesday, so no, I won't be able to come.'

The 'I would if I could, but I can't' reason for refusal can easily be seen as an excuse by the other person, and leaves an opening for them to continue to try and make you change your mind – 'Why can't you?' being the obvious opening retort. There could then follow a list of reasons/excuses countered by how these could be overcome. The other person is in effect saying 'If I can talk you out of all your excuses, you will eventually give in and do what I want.'

If a request is made to which you really cannot or do not want to comply, a way forward is to adopt the following three-point plan:

(1) Acknowledge that you have understood the request, and that you understand the other person's viewpoint.

> eg 'Yes, you do need a break away from the family, and I can see your difficulty.'

(2) Say that you can't, giving your reasons why. Keep this brief and to the point.

> eg 'I can't lend you my camper-van. I'm not insured for other drivers, and in any case, I don't lend my van to anyone – not even family.'

(3) Let the other person know that the matter is closed by actually saying 'No'.

eg '...so no, I won't let you borrow it for your holidays.'

This *should* be enough to deter further pressure. You have softened the blow of a harsh refusal by giving *some* information, and by explaining your reasons. By following these three points, you are more likely to have your refusal accepted, and to keep relationships intact.

No excuses

This is skills practice and is an optional follow-up to the activity **I would if I could, but....** Participants are asked to consider a real life situation where they have had to refuse a request, and where the outcome was less than satisfactory. Using this scenario, they will practise saying 'No' in a manner which is assertive and effective, and with which they feel comfortable.

Objectives By the end of this activity participants will:

- have practised refusing a request in a manner acceptable to them;
- have received feedback on the effectiveness of their assertiveness;
- have had the opportunity to observe colleagues, and offer advice on their ability to refuse requests in an assertive way.

Resources None.

Time 45 minutes.

Method

Step 1: Explain the activity Participants will be asked to think of a situation where they have experienced problems when saying 'No'. Alternatively, they may know of a future situation where they are going to be 'put on the spot' and will have difficulty refusing a request.

Working in groups of three, each will take a turn at explaining the situation to their colleagues, giving as much background information as possible. They will then play out the refusal as many times as is necessary for them to feel comfortable with their content, delivery,

body language and so on. Other group members should give constructive feedback and offer advice. They will look for a relaxed and confident style, an empathetic manner, and an approach which gives just enough information to explain the refusal. *Reasons* not *excuses* should be offered, and most importantly, the word 'No' must be used somewhere in the refusal.

Step 2: Explain the procedure and timings Individuals may need a few minutes to think about a real situation which they would like to practise in their group. Each group will then have approximately 10 minutes for each skills practice (30–40 minutes in all).

Step 3: Set the groups to work The same people can work together in triads (one group of four if necessary) as in the previous activity, **I would if I could, but....** Circulate around groups, reminding the observers to be constructively critical, and to offer advice to colleagues on how their approach might be improved. Add any observations of your own.

Step 4: Reconvene the main group Take comments and questions.

Step 5: Sum up and close the activity There are times when a stark refusal – 'No I won't' – may be appropriate. Some people may find that they can say 'No' in the majority of situations, without justification or apology. However, many of us experience difficulty in refusing requests unless we can 'soften the blow' for the other person. In this way, although they may be disappointed, hopefully they are not resentful. This activity was about finding a way of saying 'No' which leaves both requester and refuser feeling good about themselves.

Rejoinders

What happens when you make an assertive request, but the response is not quite what the textbooks say, or what you expected? This activity looks at how the same remark, made to separate people each with a unique relationship with you, can be received quite differently. It should be run after participants have become skilled in recognizing assertive methods of stating needs or making requests. It can be used as a stand-alone activity, or as part one of a sequence with the activities **What next?** and **Tidy that**. Running the three activities consecutively could provide a morning or afternoon workshop of 3 to 4 hours duration.

Objectives By the end of this activity participants will:

- better appreciate that learning to make honest, clear, concise, assertive requests has to take into account the relationship with the receiver.

Resources Copy of the Exercise Sheet for each participant, pen/pencils, tables, clipboards or facility for lap-top writing.

Time 30–45 minutes.

Method

Step 1: Explain the activity, procedures and timings An Exercise Sheet will be issued which has written on it 'partner', 'boss', 'son' and so on, with space beneath to record what response each is likely to give to an assertive request. The request is 'Would you tidy that please?' Working alone initially, participants should record the sort

of verbal response which would be likely in each instance, plus attitudes, body language and so on which would accompany that response. Think of different situations when you might use this request. The Exercise Sheets will not be collected in, so the information you record will remain as confidential as you want it to be. It is important that you be as honest as you can. 10 minutes will be allowed for this.

Working in triads (1 or 2 groups of 4 if there is an odd number), participants will then briefly discuss the exercise before returning to plenary to share thoughts about the activity with the rest of the group.

Step 2: Arrange chairs so that participants are in small groups. Issue a copy of the Exercise Sheet to each participant, and a pen or pencil if required Ensure that everyone has something on which to rest the Exercise Sheet – table top or clipboard.

Step 3: Begin the exercise Remind participants that they should each complete the exercise individually, but can discuss issues with others in their group. They should be as honest as possible in their responses, but it should be stressed that they need only share what they want to share with others, in small group or plenary.

Step 4: If, after 10 minutes, groups have not started discussing issues raised by the exercise, instruct them to do so Much can be gained by exchanging experiences of this kind and discovering how others might deal with difficult situations. How long is given to this aspect of the exercise depends on the course timetable, and how useful you feel the discussions are to each group. Discussions usually become anecdotal, which is fine at this stage.

Step 5: Reconvene the group. Ask if anyone would like to share with the whole group any aspect of interest arising from the activity Participants should be discouraged from anecdotal comment in the plenary session, but encouraged to share with the group observations about the activity and learning gained from it.

Questions you might use:

- Were you surprised at *how* different responses are likely to be depending on relationships, situations, etc? What did you learn from this?
- In what ways does conditioning play a part in individuals' responses to requests?

- Did you begin to share with other members of your group how you would respond to the attitude, comments and so on of the receiver in each instance?

Step 6: Close the activity referring to the objectives

This activity can be used alone or usefully followed by the activities **What next?** and **Tidy that**.

EXERCISE SHEET

Rejoinders

'Would you tidy that please?'
List below the response you are likely to get from this request, worded exactly as written, from the listed people. Some relationships may not apply to you. Ignore these. Try to imagine not only the words of the response, but attitudes, tone of voice, body language and so on that would accompany the words. If you want to record the responses of, say each child, or different subordinates separately, that is fine. Use the back of the sheet or rough paper if there is not enough room.

PARTNER

MOTHER/FATHER

CHILDREN

SISTER/BROTHER

RELATION (OTHER)

BOSS

WORK COLLEAGUE

SUBORDINATE

CLOSE FRIEND

ACQUAINTANCE

NEIGHBOUR

STRANGER

WHAT NEXT?

This activity can be run after the activity **Rejoinders** and is a follow-up to it. It pursues the theme 'what happens when you make an assertive request, but the response is not quite what you expected?' Having explored possible reactions to the request, this activity looks at individuals' typical behaviour patterns in an interaction, and considers how other approaches might have had different results.

Objectives By the end of this activity participants will:

- be better aware of their own behaviour patterns;
- have discussed, in small groups, alternative responses to difficult situations;
- be familiar with other participants' problem areas and better equipped to give constructive feedback

Resources Copy of Exercise Sheets 1 and 2 for each participant, pen/pencils, tables, clipboards or facility for lap-top writing.

Time 1½ to 2 hours.

Method

Step 1: Explain procedure for the first part of the activity Each participant will have completed the **Rejoinders** exercise, and will have begun to discuss, in their groups, reactions to the various responses to their request 'Would you tidy that please?' The next step is to complete another exercise, this time recording what they would do and say next in the dialogue with partner, boss, neighbour and so on. In other words, how would the interaction continue in normal circum-

stances. We all have conversations with ourselves, 'I'll say ... then he'll reply ... so I'll tell him...' and so on. Participants should imagine the scenario, and record how things might progress in each instance. Participants will need to work alone initially – 20 minutes will be allowed for this – but can consult with others in their group should they wish to do so. If some scenarios prove difficult, individuals should concentrate on those of most importance to them. The Exercise Sheets will not be collected in, so participants need only share what they want to share with others in the group and during plenary.

Step 2: Issue copies of, and begin, Exercise Sheet 1 Participants should stay in the same groups as in the previous activity, **Rejoinders.**

Step 3: Check on progress after 20 minutes. Negotiate more time if necessary If some participants have finished, however, move on to the next exercise. Individuals should have completed enough to progress to other parts of the activity and can, of course, finish this exercise should they wish to do so in their own time.

Step 4: Issue Exercise 2. Explain the procedure and timings Working from the previous sheets, participants should examine their responses, ie how they would normally react, what they would typically say, and so on in the given situation with that particular person. On this new Exercise Sheet, they should record how they *could* have reacted, ie what alternative *positive* approaches they could have used which might have changed the course of the interaction.

For example, if someone said to their partner 'Would you tidy that please?' and recorded a typical response of 'OK, in a minute' while the partner continued to watch TV, their typical, normal reaction might be to move up a gear (loudly) 'You said that ten minutes ago – I want that cleared *now*.' On this Exercise Sheet participants should consider different, perhaps better, approaches to this interaction.

Participants may find it beneficial to work with their group colleagues on this. Whether anything is physically recorded on the sheet is up to each individual, but it may be useful to jot down suggestions on how the communication, in each instance, might have been improved. This can then serve as an aide-mémoire.

Groups will be allowed up to 45 minutes for these discussions. A time check will be taken after 30 minutes to review progress.

Step 5: Reconvene the whole group. Ask if anyone would like to share anything of interest arising from the activity.

Questions you might use:

- Were there any disagreements between group members about alternative courses of action regarding the scenarios? Would you share these with the whole group? What do other people think of ...'s suggestion that ... ?
- How useful was it to share these situations with others?
- What were the main learning points for individuals?
- What difficulties, if any, do you see in putting this learning into practice?

Step 6: Close the activity

EXERCISE SHEET I

What next?

Using the information recorded on the **Rejoinders** exercise, record below how you think the situation might develop in normal circumstances. What are you likely to say; what is your attitude likely to be – what happens next?

PARTNER

MOTHER/FATHER

CHILDREN

SISTER/BROTHER

RELATION (OTHER)

BOSS

WORK COLLEAGUE

SUBORDINATE

CLOSE FRIEND

ACQUAINTANCE

NEIGHBOUR

STRANGER

EXERCISE SHEET 2

In the spaces below, suggest how things might have been handled differently. What could you have done or said which might have improved the interaction?

PARTNER

MOTHER/FATHER

CHILDREN

SISTER/BROTHER

RELATION (OTHER)

BOSS

WORK COLLEAGUE

SUBORDINATE

CLOSE FRIEND

ACQUAINTANCE

NEIGHBOUR

STRANGER

TIDY THAT

This activity allows participants to practice, in a supportive environment, the interactions which have been fully discussed in the previous two activities of this linked sequence: **Rejoinders** and **What next?**

Objectives By the end of this activity participants will:

- within the security of an established small group, have had the opportunity to practice at least one interaction relevant to themselves;
- have assisted a colleague by acting the role of someone known to that person during skills practice;
- have observed at least two interactions, and given constructive feedback.

Resources Copy of the Observer Sheet for each participant, pens/pencils, 'props' for authenticity (tables, chairs, magazines, rough paper – any odds and ends which constitute 'rubbish').

Time 1 hour.

Method

Step 1: Explain the procedure and timings Participants will stay within their small groups. By now everyone will be familiar with other group members' responses to the previous activities **Rejoinders** and **What next?** This is now an opportunity to practice choosing words, phrasing sentences, adopting appropriate tone of voice and body language and so on.

Participants will take it in turn to rehearse one of the interactions

they have been working on. One of their colleagues should act out the part of 'the other person' (work colleague, neighbour, sister, etc). This should not be too difficult as, after the previous activities, they will be familiar with most of the scenarios and have some idea of the way 'the other person' is likely to behave. The other member(s) of the team will observe, take notes, and give constructive feedback at the end of the interaction.

Every skills practice should begin with the words 'Would you tidy that please?' Each group member should take a turn at practising assertion skills, being observer, and taking the role of 'the other person'.

Individuals should choose which of the scenarios they wish to rehearse. If time allows, more than one interaction could be practised by each participant.

30–45 minutes will be allowed for skills practice.

Step 2: Ensure that groups have sufficient and appropriate space for their needs, and any resources they need Participants should be encouraged to make the situation as real as possible. For example, would the interaction take place sitting or standing? If the chosen scenario is in the workplace, a table may be required to simulate an office environment or a counter. 'Props' may be required for authenticity – a pile of magazines or papers.

Step 3: Issue the Observer Sheets. Begin the activity Circulate, observing and giving advice where needed.

Step 4: Check progress after 30 minutes Some groups take longer than others to fully analyse and adequately process the dialogue practice. Allow an extra 15 minutes if necessary so that every individual has had the chance to practise at least one interaction.

Step 5: Reconvene the group. Lead a short discussion to tease out the learning points.

Questions you might use:

- Which of the elements of the three activities did you find most difficult? Why?
- Which of the elements of the three activities did you find most useful? Why?
- Did anything surprise you about the communication process during the skills practice?

- Which 'role' did you find most enlightening – being yourself, being in the shoes of 'the other person', or being observer?
- What did you learn from each of these roles?
- What would be the main learning point that each of you takes from these three activities?

Step 6: Close the activity

OBSERVER SHEET

Tidy that

During the dialogue, take note of any words or phrases used which set up difficulties for the person practising assertion skills, and the result of that choice.

Similarly, make note of any positive attitudes, good responses which produced a desired effect.

Watch for body language. What did it tell you about how the interaction was going?

Notes:

Begin the feedback session by first getting the reactions of the person practising assertion skills. What did they think went well? How could the communication have been improved? Next, put the same questions to the respondent. Finally, offer constructive comments of your own.

CHAPTER 6

TRICKY SITUATIONS

NO LOSERS

An activity which looks at the options for handling conflict. Trainer input is followed by small group work to identify methods of arriving at a win/win resolution to interpersonal conflict.

Objectives By the end of this activity participants will:

- have discussed the implications of choosing various methods of handling conflict;
- have worked through case studies as a means of reinforcing learning.

Resources Copy of **Trainer's notes**, copy of the Exercise Sheet for each participant, and a copy of the Handout for each participant, paper, pens/pencils, flipchart and coloured markers.

Time 1½ hours.

Method
Step 1: Trainer input on conflict handling Write up on flipchart, and talk through, the five approaches to conflict resolution suggested in the **Trainer's notes.**

Step 2: Ask the group to identify behaviours associated with each of the five approaches Write suggestions, perhaps in a different coloured marker, against the five flipcharted headings. Discuss the implications of such behaviours.

Examples:

Against 'Withdrawal' you might have 'Stop talking to them'. The implications are that eventually there may be avoidance of contact with that person. Unresolved conflict of this sort can produce feelings of resentment; hurt that the other person hasn't guessed the reason for the communication breakdown; lowered self-esteem, and so on.

Against 'Suppression' you might have 'Act as if nothing's the matter'. But of course, something *is* the matter, and the problem will go on festering away in the mind. This could result in an unreasonable outburst at some later time – often about some unrelated and minor matter.

Against 'Win/lose' you might have 'Sulk until they give in'. This manipulative behaviour might be effective in the short term and result in a 'win', but what about the long-term implications? Does it bode well for a long and fulfilling relationship?

Step 3: Issue and go through the Handout This explains more fully the stages needed to achieve a win/win solution.

Step 4: Divide the group into small groups of 3 or 4 people. Issue and explain the Exercise Sheet. Set groups to work There are three case studies for the groups to work through. They should discuss fully, then suggest approaches matching each of the five outlined above, paying particular attention, of course, to finding a win/win solution. The point of the activity is *not* to become an expert in suppression or win/lose techniques!

Participants will need to hypothesise about the scenarios in order to offer approaches to the conflict situations.

Step 5: Check with the groups after about 20 minutes. Negotiate more time if necessary Circulate during this time, clarifying and assisting where necessary.

Step 6: Reconvene the main group. Go through each group's suggestions paying particular attention to their proposed win/win solution

For example, a win/win solution to the first case study would be for one student to use the mashed insides of baked potatoes to make a Shepherd's Pie, while the other deep-fries the 'jackets' to serve stuffed or with a dip. Alternatively, both students and guests could eat together.

The point of asking groups to offer responses under each of the headings is to reinforce awareness of inappropriate as well as appropriate behaviour. While some time needs to be spent on 'unpacking' this part of the exercise, it is far more important to ensure that participants understand the stages required to bring about a win/win result.

Step 7: Sum up, then close the activity referring to the objectives It will not always be possible to arrive at a win/win solution. Neither will it always be appropriate. Different reactions will suit different situations at different times with different people. As with other areas of assertiveness, conflict handling is about choosing appropriate behaviour to meet existing needs.

TRAINER'S NOTES

No losers

There are several ways we can react to interpersonal conflict. The extremes are confrontation or avoidance – the fight or flight responses. Most participants will recognize which of the following behaviours they habitually display:

Withdrawal People who hate confrontations which might result in the other person's anger, sarcasm, rejection and so on, withdraw from the situation rather than face up to it. They are usually sensitive to their own and others' feelings, and don't want to hurt or be hurt. By implication, the other person invariably 'wins'.

Suppression These people suppress their own needs, opinions, feelings and so on. Their attitude is 'anything for a quiet life' or 'peace at any price'. The other person invariably 'wins'.

Win/lose At the other end of the spectrum, there are those who see interpersonal conflict as a challenge in which there has to be a winner and loser. This may be motivated by self-preservation, but the outcome is usually a battle in which relationships might suffer. The stronger party – usually the more aggressive – emerges the 'winner'.

Compromise At first sight, this may seem the most favourable option. In some cases it is the best solution possible; but with both sides giving a little, through negotiation, in order to gain *something*, often the *best* solution is not achieved – rather a watered-down version of the ideal. At worst, both parties may feel cheated and dissatisfied with the outcome.

Win/win If it can be achieved, the ideal solution is one where both parties emerge as winners. This is not always possible to achieve, but it is what everyone should work towards. By defining both party's needs, then trying to equitably meet those needs while supporting and respecting both people's values, a win/win solution can often be achieved. Relationships are maintained, and can even be enhanced by this process.

EXERCISE SHEET

No losers

Below are three case studies. In your groups, suggest five approaches to resolving each of these conflict situations; one reflecting withdrawal, a second reflecting suppression, a third – win/lose, a fourth – compromise, and finally (and most importantly) a win/win solution.

(1) Two students, Ben and Martin, share a flat and all the expenses. It is the end of term and their grants are almost spent – they are, in fact, broke. Unknown to the other, each has invited a friend round for a meal, aware of the fact that there are two largish potatoes left in the food cupboard. Both want the potatoes to form the basis of the meal.

(2) John (a surveyor) and Beth (a solicitor) have one small child, Emily. Before starting a family, they both agreed that they would continue working, and share household and child-minding responsibilities. Normally, either John or Beth takes Emily to a child-minder in the morning before driving to work, and they take it in turns to collect her later in the day. Last night (Sunday) they had to call the doctor because Emily was fractious, and had developed a rash. Chickenpox was diagnosed. John says he has three properties to survey on Monday and can't spare the time to stay at home with the child. Beth is due in court.

(3) A local charitable group applied for a grant from the local authority, and were thrilled when a substantial one-off amount was awarded. The Secretary wants the money to be spent on administrative equipment – a word processor and photocopier. The treasurer feels that the money would be better spent on a publicity launch and fund-raising events.

HANDOUT

No losers

Resolving conflict in an assertive manner requires problem solving skills. Too often we are 'reactive' when interpersonal conflict threatens, when it would be preferable to be 'proactive'. In other words, we act instinctively, whether the instinct be to become aggressively competitive, or to back off to avoid a scene. Far better to establish the facts of the situation – what the other person's feelings and needs are, how they compare with our own, and so on. By adopting the latter, proactive approach, there is far more likelihood of a win/win outcome.

To initiate this pro-active approach we need to:

- find out what the other person needs; what they want to gain from the situation; how strong their feelings are about the situation, and so on;
- compare this with our own needs, feelings, wants and expectations;
- establish where there are similarities, differences and where the needs might dovetail;
- look at the options; discuss and evaluate;
- co-operate; look together for a win/win solution.

Open dialogue is a requisite of this approach, as are good negotiating skills, together with the ability and willingness to recognize the other person's basic rights while not neglecting our own. Think of the situation as a problem solving exercise rather than interpersonal conflict; the other person as a partner, not as an opponent.

CONFLICT RESOLUTION

This activity should follow **No losers.** It reinforces the learning which has taken place during the previous activity by relating the issues raised to participants' own situations.

Objectives By the end of this activity participants will:

- have discussed with one other person an interpersonal conflict which has been less than successful, or a current conflict situation where practice is called for;
- have considered the various options, their benefits and drawbacks in the given situation;
- have rehearsed initiating a discussion with a view to reaching a win/win resolution;
- have given and received feedback on resolving conflict.

Resources (*Optional*) – Copy of participants' personal training programme from **Ladder of success**. Copies of the Handout from **No losers**, copy of the **Trainer's notes** from **No losers**, flipchart and marker.

Time 1 hour.

Method
Step 1: Explain the activity This is a follow-up to **No losers**. Participants will apply the learning of that activity to their own situations. Working in pairs, they will identify a past confrontation where they had not behaved as assertively as they would have liked, or alternatively, discuss a planned exchange where interpersonal conflict

might occur. They should work together to plan an effective exchange, aiming for a win/win resolution to the problem.

Step 2: Remind the group of the five approaches to handling conflict as outlined in No losers See **No losers – Trainer's notes**. It would help if the headings were flipcharted.

Step 3: Instruct participants to spend a few minutes deciding on an area of conflict or potential conflict in their lives on which they would like to work If participants have made a personal plan from which to work, listing and prioritizing areas in their lives where they would like to be more assertive (as recommended in the activity, **Ladder of success**), they may well find a situation here on which to work.

Step 4: Divide the group into pairs (one triad if there is an odd number). Explain the procedure and timings Participants should take one situation at a time and work through it together. The 'owner' of the situation will need to brief her/his partner, giving background information and relevant details about 'the other person' in the conflict. She or he should describe how they dealt with, or would normally deal with, potential conflict of this kind. Partners should discuss the options (under the five headings) and the implications of taking such action. They should discuss the benefits and drawbacks to each choice, eg whether, in the circumstances, suppression might be the best policy, or whether compromise through negotiation is the best that situation could offer.

Wherever possible, however, a win/win solution should be looked for. Pairs should rehearse their approaches, using the Handout from **No losers** as a guide. Initially, 15 minutes will be allowed for the discussion and rehearsal of each participant's situation – 30 minutes in all.

(More time should be allowed if there is a triad, so that each participant has the opportunity to discuss a personal potentially confrontational situation.)

Step 5: Renegotiate times if necessary. Reconvene the main group for a plenary discussion It may be that some pairs would want advice from other members of the main group, or reassurance that the option decided on in their situation is the right one. However, ultimately the only person who knows what the 'right' approach is, will be the 'owner' of the problem. Stress that assertiveness is about choice of

behaviours. A win/win solution, though ideal, may not always be appropriate for a certain situation or with a certain person, or, indeed, at this particular time.

Step 6: Close the activity by referring to the objectives

DISCREPANCY

This is a role-play activity. It is intended to give participants a 'feel' for the skills required in pointing out a discrepancy between what was thought to have been agreed, and what in fact actually happened. As with all role-plays, it is crucial that this activity be followed by skills practice where participants test out the techniques learnt on simulations relevant to their personal needs.

Objectives By the end of this activity participants will:

- have practised the skills involved in assertively pointing out a discrepancy;
- have assisted a colleague by participating in a role-play, and by giving constructive feedback on technique.

Resources Flipchart and marker, copy of the Exercise Sheet for each participant, copy of the Observer Sheet for each participant, materials needed for role-play, chairs, tables, notepaper, etc.

Time 45 minutes to one hour.

Method

Step 1: Explain the purpose of the activity, procedure and timings (see description above) This will be a role-play activity. In pairs, participants will act out roles to practise the skill of dealing with discrepancies in an assertive manner.

When participants are comfortable with the technique, they will be given the opportunity to rehearse exchanges relevant to their own situations.

We must all have experienced a situation where we *think* that we've been heard and understood, *believe* we have confirmed that something will happen in a certain way, *assume* that the other person agreed to deadlines and so on, then discover that things have been done a different way – or not at all. The result is a dilemma. Do we confront the situation and risk conflict? Do we keep quiet and hope everything will sort itself out without our intervention? Or do we adopt an assertive approach?

Working in groups of three (four if there is an odd number) participants take it in turn to act out roles, or observe interactions and offer constructive feedback to colleagues. Each role-play, including feedback, should take no longer than 5 minutes.

Step 3: Allocate participants to sub-groups of 3 or 4 Use any method to do this.

Step 4: Issue the Exercise Sheet and Observer Sheets While distributing these documents, explain that the Exercise Sheet has a choice of scenarios for groups to act out. Individuals should choose the situation with which they feel most comfortable, or which is nearest to their own experience, for their role-play practice. If possible, different role-plays should be practised within the sub-groups. However, if two people want to act out the same scenario, that's fine. Often extra learning can be gained by seeing someone else's handling of a similar situation.

Step 5: Allow participants a few minutes to read through the scenarios. Explain that they will rotate within the group, taking it in turns to practise assertion, role-play 'the other person' and to observe and give feedback The observer(s) should concentrate on the words, tone of voice, body language, of the person practising assertion, not the other 'actor'.

Step 6: Ensure that groups have the resources needed for their role-plays. Begin the activity Circulate amongst groups, observing and giving advice on procedure if necessary, but avoid commenting on the role-plays at this stage. Check to see that the five minute rule is being observed, ie ensure that everyone has had the chance to practise assertive behaviour before reconvening the group.

Step 7: After 15–20 minutes – when everyone has practised assertion at least once – reconvene the group for a plenary discussion of learning points.

Questions you might use:

- If this had been real life, would anyone's natural reaction to any of the scenarios have been to leave well alone and hope that things would sort themselves, somehow, without your intervention?
- How did you cope with the role-plays? Did you find the practice easy or difficult? Why?
- What was the easiest part? What was the most difficult?
- What sorts of issues arose in the first scenario – the late arrival of the furniture? (Use similar questioning with the other three simulations.)
- Which role did you find the most enlightening – practising assertion, being 'the other person' or being observer?
- What did you learn from the role-plays?

Step 8: Sum up, adding any observations of your own When challenging discrepancies, the assertive approach is to keep to the facts, eg 'this is what we agreed', 'this is what I expected'. Be straightforward, make no apologies, do not accuse or blame. Talk about the situation, not personalities. Ascertain whether there is a problem beyond the control of the other person which might account for the discrepancy. Allow them to respond. Only when you have full knowledge of the facts will you be able to assess how to best handle the situation.

Step 9: Close the activity

EXERCISE SHEET

Discrepancy

Choose from one of the following scenarios for practising your assertion skills:

(1) You are expecting delivery of some furniture. The salesperson informed you that it would be dispatched on Wednesday morning. You have taken the morning off from work to receive this furniture. It is now 2 p.m. and there is no sign of the delivery.

(2) This morning you sent an important letter to the secretariat department for typing. You informed the typist that you needed it returned by 2.30 p.m. in time to amend if necessary, and be ready for the afternoon postal collection (in fact, to be doubly sure, you attached a note to the work to that effect). The last collection at work is at 4.00 p.m. It is now 3.15 p.m., and your typed letter has not been returned.

(3) You have a young neighbour who spends much of the time out of the house, but when he's at home, is not the quietest of people! You have talked the issue through with him, and have agreed that music levels will be kept tolerably low (you, too, like to play your music loudly on occasion) and at a minimum after 10.30 p.m. at night. So far, the agreement has been kept, but it's now 11.45 p.m. and it sounds as if a herd of elephants has arrived next door – not music, but loud voices, thumps and crashes. This has been going on for more than 15 minutes.

(4) You have to write a report for the finance committee meeting. It has to be duplicated and sent out with the agenda in two days' time. You have to rely on data and statistics produced by various people, one of whom is your boss who has still not delivered the information you require, although you've asked her on several occasions, and explained your

deadlines. If you don't get this vital information from her within the next hour or so, you will find it impossible to produce the report within normal office hours.

When it's your turn to play 'the other person', try to think of as many logical reasons, as well as excuses, why the furniture has not been delivered or the letter typed; for the noise level; or why the statistics haven't been provided as requested. In other words, don't make the task easy for the person who is practising assertion skills.

OBSERVER SHEET

Discrepancy

During the dialogue, take note of any words or phrases used which set up difficulties for the person practising assertion skills, and the result of that choice.

Similarly, make note of any positive attitudes, and good responses which produced a desired effect.

Watch for body language. What did it tell you about how the interaction was going?

Notes:

Begin the feedback session by first getting the reactions of the person practising assertion skills. What did they think went well? How could the communication have been improved? Next ask the same questions of the respondent before adding constructive observations of your own.

THINK POSITIVE

This activity encourages participants to rethink and rephrase statements turning them from negative, reactive observations to positive, thoughtful assertions.

Objectives By the end of this activity participants will:

- have practised looking objectively at negative thoughts and actions, turning them around to offer more creative responses.

Resources Copy of the Exercise Sheet for each participant, pen/pencils, notepaper.

Time 30 minutes to one hour.

Method

Step 1: Introduce the activity This activity gives participants the opportunity to look at a few off-the-peg situations; to give them some thought and suggest ways in which negativity can be turned around into a learning experience. For example, if you say to yourself 'I'm always late', this is not only negative thinking, but can become a self-fulfilling prophesy. Keep thinking like this, and you *will* always be late. Subconsciously, you have accepted a fault and given yourself permission to indulge in it!

A better way of dealing with this is firstly to recognize the situation: 'OK, I accept I have a problem with timekeeping'. This is not ignoring or merely accepting the situation, but the next step to positive, creative thinking, 'I'm not pleased with myself; what can I do to ensure that I arrive at meetings on time?' From here, strategies can be worked out and tried, to solve the timekeeping problem.

Often, too, we have our own preconceived ideas about what is right and wrong, and measure others against our own yardstick. We either find them wanting, or feel that we can never possibly be as good as, as attractive as, as articulate as ... and so on. The same principle applies. Look at each situation for what it is, acknowledge how you feel about it, then move on to see what can be done about it; how you can prevent it happening again; now that this has failed, what is still possible and so on.

Step 2: Explain the procedure and timings for the activity Each participant will be given an Exercise Sheet on which is written 12 statements. In small groups they will discuss each statement, and suggest how negativity can be turned into positive thought or action (15 minutes). This will be followed by a short plenary discussion.

Step 3: Issue the Exercise Sheet, pens/pencils and notepaper if required. Divide the group into small groups of 3 or 4. Begin the activity Encourage groups to come up with as many positive options for each statement as they can.

Step 4: After 15 minutes, or when groups have completed the task, reconvene the main group for plenary discussion Ask a group in turn to lead on offering suggestions for thought or action on each of the situations presented. Discuss the pros and cons of each, encouraging assertive and positive responses. For example, suggestions for the first statement could include 'ask other friends to share the meal'; 'freeze the food for another occasion'; 'be grateful for the spare hours to do other things'; 'look on the episode as a learning experience – you now know how to prepare that particular meal in advance'.

You could also discuss the advantages of proactive responses over reactive ones. Continuing with the above example, rather than curse and complain about others' lack of consideration, or throwing the meal in the bin, far better to see what positive thoughts and actions can emerge from a potentially negative situation. It is usually preferable to give situations some thought, considering every aspect, possible consequences, rather than to act impulsively.

Step 5: Sum up, then close the activity Every one of us has negative thoughts, but with practice these can be recognized and turned into positive statements or actions. This negativity can be about our own abilities or feelings, or may refer to others who upset us, or do not conform to our own standards. This is perfectly normal and natural,

but it benefits self and others if we can take stock of these feelings, thoughts, or statements, look at them objectively, learn from them, and change them into more creative responses.

EXERCISE SHEET

Think positive

In your groups, discuss each of the following situations. Suggest positive ways forward, whether this involves thought (self-talk) or action.

(1) 'I prepared all the food yesterday; now this morning they've rung and said they can't come.'
(2) 'How dare she keep taking me for granted!'
(3) 'Why does all this work have to be done by yesterday, just to meet his deadlines?'
(4) 'I shouldn't have done that. What a stupid mistake.'
(5) 'I'll never be able to do this – I'd better leave it.'
(6) 'I ate far too much today.'
(7) 'I'm afraid to ask; what if she says "No"?'
(8) 'But I always do it this way!'
(9) 'After all the time and effort we've put into this contract – and now they've cancelled!'
(10) 'If I agree to do the presentation, and it goes badly, the organization will suffer.'
(11) 'I've been asked to stand in for Henry. There's no way I'll be as good. He's so distinguished.'
(12) Oh no, here comes Tracey! She goes on and on about what she would do if she were in my shoes.'

POSITIVE ACTION

This activity would usefully follow **Think positive**, although it can stand alone. It encourages participants to examine their thoughts and actions on a daily basis and to transform negativity into a learning experience.

Objectives By the end of this activity participants will:

- begin to evaluate thoughts, statements and actions, on a regular basis, and turn potential problems or areas of negativity into opportunities;
- have been given a means to enhance interpersonal skills and feelings of self-worth.

Resources None.

Time Notes should be taken in participants' own time.

Method
Step 1: Give a short explanation of how negative attitudes to self and others can be recognized and turned into positive thought or action
Daily, every one of us has negative thoughts about ourselves – our appearance, attributes, what we said or didn't say, and so on. We can dwell on mistakes, agonize over perceived insensitivity or thoughtlessness, seethe about injustices – in other words, wind ourselves up, allowing ourselves no outlet (apart from the occasional outburst when things get too much). Even the most placid have thoughts such as 'I must get more exercise' (implicitly implying 'I'm out of condition – or getting fat!') or 'She really is an awkward so-and-so' (indicating a

communication problem, of whoever's making). Most of us set ourselves impossible yardsticks which we cannot hope to live up to every minute of every day. Also, we often judge people by our own standards and feel annoyed when we find others wanting.

How much better to learn to recognize these feelings, as they happen, to learn from them, and try to turn negative thoughts and actions into positive ones.

The secret is to identify our own negative perceptions, examine them objectively, learn from them, and decide on positive alternatives or options. For example, if you have been put in charge of a new department and have feelings of inadequacy – 'John was an excellent leader; how will I ever match up?' – acknowledge that yes, John set a high standard, but John is John and you are you with your own skills, attributes and strengths. The department may be run differently, but just as efficiently under your command. If you are fed up with your partner saying he will do a certain thing, but that thing never happens, recognize the situation for what it is, acknowledge your feelings about it, then go about building strategies for coping – 'What else can I try to encourage him to...' or 'Okay; what's the alternative if he doesn't ... what other options are open to me?' Negative feeling then becomes positive action.

Step 2: Explain the activity The success of this activity depends on how much work participants are prepared to do, in their own time, to practise recognizing their own negativity and turning it around.

Use a diary or notebook to record – on a daily basis – negative feelings and problem situations. To begin with, you will probably only recognize the 'biggies' like 'I nearly blew a fuse when Marketing changed their figures for a third time' or 'I implied to Jerry that he was selfish; I didn't mean that, and feel awful now'. Thoughts about yourself are usually more subtle, more frequent, and less easy to recognize – 'Gosh, I look my age today!', but are equally important.

Each evening or when you have some spare time, consider each entry. The first step is to acknowledge the situation. It *did* happen; you *did* feel like that – criticizing, fighting, repressing or regretting it doesn't change anything. Accept that you felt angry, upset, hurt or fed up; accept the problem *as it was/is*. Now you are ready to learn from it and suggest to yourself what you can do to change your thinking, or to turn the problem into an opportunity. Be receptive to what *might be*.

For example, take 'Gosh, I look my age today!'. This depressed me; so what shall I do? Accept it and continue to go around feeling awful? No. So what are my options? Acknowledge the fact that I *am* getting older – everyone is, and there's nothing that can be done about that. So consider ways I might alter or improve my appearance. More sleep? A different hair style? Smile more often and learn to love my 'laughter lines'?

Step 3: (If this session is run as part of a training programme) Participants should bring the diary or notebook to the next session. In small groups, discuss the entries. Other group members may be able to suggest alternative strategies.

If appropriate, observations can also be shared with the main group.

Step 4: Sum up the activity This activity suggests a way forward for participants to enhance feelings of self-worth. It should also improve interpersonal skills. Diary/notebook entries should be kept for as long as felt helpful by individuals.

OFF THE PEG

This activity differs from others in the book, in concept, and therefore in layout. It offers 100 off-the-peg role-play situations covering several areas of assertiveness training. As has been stressed throughout, wherever possible participants should practise assertiveness skills on 'real' situations – ones which are personal, and therefore relevant and helpful to individuals. However, there are times – when learning new techniques for example – when scenarios need to be set which are non-challenging *because* they are not personal. It goes without saying that this is a selection to dip into. Some are work-related, others are more general. Choose the ones that best fit the purpose of a particular training session. There are several ways these scenarios can be used:

- individuals could write assertive responses;
- there could be small group discussion of the scenarios;
- passive, aggressive and assertive responses might be considered;
- the situations could be acted out in small groups with protagonists and observers;
- volunteers could act out the situations in front of the whole group with participant and trainer feedback.

Where possible, the scenarios have been put into categories. There will be some overlap, however, and some situations may be used to practise various techniques. Number 1, for example, could be making a request – to your boss to travel to the conference separately, or to Paul to drive considerately, or to colleagues so that you can sit in the front passenger seat. It could equally well be used to practise offering criticism, or Broken Record. Feel free to use the situations in any way you prefer.

100 SCENARIOS

Off the peg

Making requests

(1) You have to travel to a conference with three colleagues. Paul is going to drive (he has a company car). You suffer from travel sickness. Paul is a poor driver (swerving about the road, taking risks, using fast acceleration and abrupt braking).

(2) Ask someone not to smoke in your house.

(3) Since the office went 'open plan' you have found it difficult to write reports, plan presentations and so on because of the noise and disturbance. You would like a quiet area designated.

(4) A friend allows her children to run riot in her own house, so they do the same in yours. You want this to stop.

(5) You work in a health club. The rules say that no food or drink should be taken into the swimming pool area. An elderly gentleman carries his beer to the side of the pool where he starts to dry his young grandson with a towel.

(6) You agree to represent your fellow workers in the machine room where, in your opinion, machinery noise warrants the issuing of protective earmuffs.

(7) You want more 'space' in your relationship.

(8) You would like to eat out tonight.

(9) You want more information from your GP about a prescribed course of treatment.

(10) You are attracted to Chris and would like to ask for a date.

Refusing a request

(11) You agreed to a date, but realize now that you are not physically attracted to Lee and don't want to go out again.

(12) You are tired of having your lunch break ruined by Joan's constant chattering. You decide to have some peace and quiet by spending the hour at a lunch time concert at the local church. 'Great, I'll come too' she says.

(13) A close relative telephones. 'I hear that Ted and Mavis will be visiting you on Sunday? As it happens, I'll be in your area. I'd love to see them – and you of course.' You will be entertaining Ted and Mavis, but they really don't get on with the one telephoning. Meetings always result in arguments and bad feelings.

(14) You've never got on well with your boss. In fact, he's made your life miserable on a number of occasions. You are overjoyed to hear he has got a new job, but are then asked what you will be contributing to his leaving present.

(15) A man calls at your door collecting for charity. You are hard up this week, and are not particularly committed to this charity anyway.

(16) You and a friend enter a restaurant and take a table next to the window. The restaurant has plenty of spare tables, but the waiter asks you to move to a table for two situated in a dark corner. You ask if the table you are sitting at is reserved. It is not, and you don't want to move.

(17) The employee who used to deliver the day's takings to the bank has retired. Your boss asks you to take on this job, but you are concerned about security, and don't want the extra responsibility.

(18) You are in charge of the clerical and administrative staff at a school. The policy is that leave can only be taken during school vacations. Gwen has asked to take three weeks' holiday in the middle of the autumn term.

(19) It's only Tuesday, and your son has spent his week's allowance. He wants an advance.

(20) You do not have full double glazing. A pleasant woman calls at your house asking if you would answer a few simple questions for market research. You agree, but it soon becomes obvious that she is selling double glazing.

Setting limits

(21) A neighbour's child asks you if you will sponsor her on a marathon swim in aid of her school fund. You see that other neighbours on her list have agreed to pay for every length of the baths she completes. You can't afford this – it could run into a lot of money – but you like the child and don't want to disappoint her.

(22) A work colleague seems very friendly, but you find some of her questioning intrusive and nosey. Today she gives you some warning of what is to come when she says 'Can I ask you something personal?'

(23) You are asked to take on and complete a project by Friday. You know that to do it properly, ten days' work is involved.

(24) One member of your team is making too many personal telephone calls.

(25) A colleague has parked in your reserved space yet again.

(26) You share a house – and the chores – with two friends, but somehow it's invariably you who washes up and tidies the kitchen.

(27) You are on a date and want to 'go Dutch'. Your escort insists on paying the bill.

(28) During the school holidays your children always seem to have their friends at your house while you are out at work. They never seem to visit. Consequently it is your fridge which gets emptied; your rooms which are dusty and muddled; your patience which is stretched at the end of a long working day.

(29) You are prepared frequently to visit an elderly relative, but he wants to tie you down to an exact time and day each week.

(30) You readily agreed to look after a neighbour's dog while they were away on long day's business trip. The next time they asked – about a month later – you agreed again. Today they say 'OK for you to look after Pongo again tomorrow?' You resent being taken for granted.

Criticisms

(31) A new member of your team is critical of the way you run the section, and of the work of his colleagues. Morale is getting low.

(32) You have been having one or two problems in your private life. Your boss accuses you of 'being down' and says 'I'm fed up with your moods; why can't you be more sociable?'

(33) It seems that every time you begin a conversation with friends, your partner interrupts your stories to correct detail.

(34) When your partner asks what you want to do with your weekends, you invariably say that you don't mind and leave it up to her/him. Today they respond with, 'You never make decisions, but whatever I choose to do is always wrong!'

(35) One of your colleagues says 'I don't think you've been a very supportive training course member.'

(36) You have to give an appraisal interview. Your subordinate is making good progress but still makes careless mistakes.

(37) Your boss criticizes you for something that you know without a doubt you didn't do.

(38) Your typist brings in letters for you to sign. There are four mistakes on the first page alone.

(39) It is up to you to tell an employee about a personal hygiene problem.

(40) You feel strongly about the work of a charity you support and give as much time as possible to the cause. A friend challenges this and says 'You are overly concerned – there are other more worthwhile things you could do with your time.'

Put-downs

(41) Your partner gets home before you. As you come through the door you are greeted with an angry, 'Why on earth did you leave the grill on all day?'

(42) You have bought a new outfit and are about to go out wearing the new clothes. Your friend/partner says 'Where on earth did you get that? It does absolutely nothing for you.'

(43) 'Do you think you are intelligent enough to cope with this job?'

(44) You state your well thought out views clearly at the staff meeting. One of your colleagues says, 'How ridiculous; you can't be serious! That's got as much chance of working as I have of becoming Pope!'

(45) 'Every time I try to discuss things with you, you become defensive or sarcastic.'

(46) 'You'd better double check. You're such a twit – you always get the dates wrong.'

(47) 'Is there any reason why you've left this piece of cheese to fester in the back of the fridge?'

(48) 'What a stupid thing to say! Tact must be your middle name!'

(49) 'I know you're a bit slow in picking things up, so I've written the instructions out in easy stages for you, so that you can't go wrong.'

(50) 'Is everyone in this company as inefficient as you?'

Rights

(51) It's your birthday and your friends want to arrange a big party with a disco. You want to celebrate your special day in a quite different way.

(52) You live just around the corner from your place of work. Others have trains to catch so you end up being the one responsible for dealing with late customers, clearing away and closing up.

(53) You feel very strongly about a certain cause. Others at work ridicule your views.

(54) You are appalled at the bill for repairs to your car. You challenge the mechanic, and are treated, by him, as an incompetent who knows nothing about the intricacies of the work involved.

(55) It is 5.15 p.m. on Friday. Your boss is leaving for her annual vacation and is giving you hurried instructions on what to do in her absence. One of the jobs is new to you, and you don't understand the procedure.

(56) A new member of the team has a hearing disability. He is employed to do exactly the same work as you, but because of his disability your boss says he can't answer the telephone – you'll have to do that part of his job for him. As the calls are almost all complaints, you feel that this reallocation of tasks is unfair.

(57) You are talking to someone on a matter of great importance to you. Their body language tells you that they are not really listening to you.

(58) You've had a fraught year, and want to spend this Christmas quietly, at home. You have to tell your usual companions (parents, children, relations, friends) that you want this time alone.

(59) One of your colleagues at work has an annoying habit. Whatever the subject you are trying to discuss, he butts in with observations of his own, often irrelevant to the topic under discussion.

(60) One of your friends seems to resent your success – the fact that business is booming, you have a newer car, can afford better holidays and so on. He is still friendly, but continually makes remarks about your success which are sarcastic and hurtful.

Compliments

(61) You really appreciate the thoughtfulness of a colleague, but until now have never told them.

(62) You are impressed by how an employee handles a difficult client. You had previously thought him to be weak and ineffective.

(63) You have been invited to stay with a friend's relatives and realize that they've gone to a lot of extra time and effort to make you welcome.

(64) Your boss, never usually complimentary, goes out of his way to praise you for a piece of work.

(65) 'I wonder if I could ask a favour; you've always been so generous.'

Self-esteem

(66) Using a local newspaper, select a 'Situations Vacant' advert. How would you sell yourself for the post?

(67) 'Write' a Situations Wanted advert for yourself, selling your skills and attributes.

(68) You are asked at an appraisal interview why you consider yourself ready for promotion.

(69) You've been in your present job for two years, and feel ready to take on more responsibility.

(70) Your boss wants to give a job you've been working on to someone else. You consider that you've been doing a good job on it.

Money matters

(71) You work for a small private company and have not had a rise for 18 months. Comparable posts in industry earn considerably more than you, so you feel justified in asking for a raise.

(72) After receiving a favourable verbal estimate for laying a new wood-block floor in your dining room (the builder also happens to be the husband of a friend) you commission the work. Labour had been estimated at between £100 and £150. When the final invoice arrives, the total labour cost is £465. The builder explains about the extra work incurred due to difficulties in taking up the old floor, but you had neither expected – nor can you afford – the additional expense.

(73) You are a keen amateur photographer. A friend has asked you to take some photographs that she can use to make greetings cards for sale on a charity stall. You are not sure whether she is prepared to pay for the cost of the films, the processing and printing – or whether she is aware of how much expense this will entail. You are prepared to help only if she meets these costs in full.

(74) A friend has borrowed some money from you, promising to pay you back in a few days. A week has passed, and you need the cash.

(75) A group from work decide to go swimming in the lunch hour. You are the only one who drives to work, and as the swimming pool is two miles away, you use your car to get there and back. You've been going for five weeks now, and no one has mentioned helping out with petrol costs.

Harassment

(76) Because you are younger than most at your place of work and the only man to deliver post to rooms full of women, you are teased a lot, especially by one woman who calls you her toy boy and pets you a lot in front of her colleagues. This embarrasses and upsets you.

(77) You don't mind a joke, but one man goes a bit too far. Because you are petite and called Sue, he's started to call you 'his little Screw'. You find his remarks offensive.

(78) You are the only woman working in a section with eight men. At first, they watched their language and kept anecdotes and jokes to themselves. As you become more accepted as part of the team, they include you in their more ribald conversations. You find their attitude to women offensive, and decide to assert your right, as a woman, to be treated with respect.

(79) You have joined an exercise class. The instructor invariably uses you to help demonstrate how to correctly use the gym equipment. This needs physical contact, but you are aware, from his touch, of the hidden message that this contact is sending!

(80) One of your staff has obviously got a crush on you – keeps making you cakes or chocolates, fusses over making your tea and coffee and stands just too close for you to feel comfortable.

Miscellaneous

(81) Your partner has a friend who is a single parent. She calls at your home, and expects you to entertain the children while she and your partner have a quiet chat.

(82) You are having difficulty making ends meet on your present housekeeping budget and need to talk with your partner about it.

(83) Although you are a senior partner in your small business, your colleagues – all women – expect you to always put out the 'wheelie-bin' of rubbish for weekly collection.

(84) You are the manager of a small precision engineering company. The owner has decided to move location – from the city to a new

industrial development in the countryside 300 miles away – to reduce overheads. It is your responsibility to inform/consult the staff.

(85) You are the only woman on a committee. When the tea is brought in, the tray is always put in front of you for you to distribute around the table. You resent this.

(86) You are trying to give serious instructions to a colleague, who keeps fooling about, interrupting with jokey comments.

(87) Others in your department talk openly about their private lives, so it is well known that one has family responsibilities, one belongs to several sports clubs, another goes to evening classes and so on. Because you say little about yourself, it is assumed by your boss that you have more time to see late clients, work overtime to keep projects on schedule, take extra work home and so on.

(88) You strongly oppose the views of a colleague who says, 'People who deliberately make themselves homeless don't deserve and shouldn't get any state support.'

(89) Your partner has spent a lot of money on what you consider to be a hideous shirt for your Christmas present. You want to exchange it for something of your choice.

(90) Redundancies and natural wastage means a redistribution of work for everyone. The managerial level above you no longer exists, so your own workload and level of responsibility has considerably increased. You have to delegate many of your duties to other members of your team, some of whom are reluctant to do more for the same pay.

(91) You have a shared drive across which your neighbour persistently parks her car.

(92) You are offended by an acquaintance's snobbery. He says, 'I don't know how you can approve of state education. I boarded at Woedene, and expect Tristan and Sasha to do the same. We pay for the best education, mix with the right people, belong to the most exclusive clubs ... to give them the right start in life.'

(93) You agree to go to a dinner party with your partner, but are totally excluded from the conversation which centres around business and golf.

(94) 'For God's sake, we're not made of money! Whatever made you think we could afford that?'

(95) You are at the ballet, and the person in front of you leans forward in his seat, completely blocking your view of the stage.

(96) Every Thursday night your neighbours have visitors; the same ones each week, who are noisy, stay until gone midnight, and then say

lengthy goodbyes on the doorstep. They shout final farewells from their car before roaring off into the night. After a hard day, followed by your assertiveness class, you find this a bit much!

(97) A friend has agreed to do some work for you (typing, icing a birthday cake, your accounts, mending a wedding outfit). She's done her best, but it really isn't good enough and you haven't the time or money to get it redone.

(98) You've worked really hard on a presentation and had a difficult time persuading the client, but nevertheless have achieved the contract. Your boss's remark? 'Beginner's luck.'

(99) You are standing on a crowded bus. A blind person, carrying a large parcel, gets on at the next stop and stands next to you. No one offers him a seat.

(100) 'Why on earth do you want to do assertiveness training?'

CHAPTER 7

Relaxation

Relaxation 1

Most people benefit from practising relaxation techniques. Those nervous or anxious can learn to develop inner strengths from relaxation; others who get 'wound up' and tense can learn to 'unwind' and control the tension. Feelings of aggression can be calmed and stress relieved through appropriate relaxation methods. However, no one technique suits everyone, so there follows a selection of ideas which can be pursued with participants. Why not try a different one at the end of each session/day, or practise one technique, say, before role-plays, to help relax the group.

Objectives By the end of this activity participants will:

- have learnt and practised a technique for tension control;
- be able to assess whether this method might be appropriate for their own needs.

Resources Upright chairs, a few old books or telephone directories.

Time 10 minutes.

Method

Step 1: Explain the technique This is a well-known method of relaxation, but one with which some people have difficulty. Often we

are so tense, panicky, anxious or wound up that we feel unable to spare the time just to sit and relax, but this is exactly what this activity asks you to do – sit, for a few minutes, concentrating on eliminating tension from the muscles. This method, if it can be perfected, allows most of us to relax for a few moments in the working day. It does not require lying on the floor, or obvious stretching – in fact, no one need know you are consciously applying a relaxation technique. It can be practised at home, in the office, in a car (pull into a lay-by and apply the handbrake first) – even in the loo if all else fails!

Step 2: Set up the activity Participants should sit in an upright chair, with the small of the back pressed tightly into the back of the chair for support. Feet should be flat on the floor, and thighs parallel to the floor. Shorter participants may need to put an old book or telephone directory under their feet for comfort. There should be no tension on the ankles. Hands should be loose in the lap.

Step 3: Talk participants through the relaxation technique

(1) A lot of tension is felt in the neck and shoulders, so first, gently stretch out the neck muscles by slowly lowering your head to the right shoulder, then back to the vertical, then down to the left shoulder. Don't be alarmed if you hear scrunching noises – most people do! Repeat this a couple more times, then let the head drop gently on to the chest, and return it to the vertical. Do this a couple of times. If the muscles still feel very tense, lower chin to chest and very gently rock your head from side to side. **Never** try to roll the head in a complete circle. The bones of the neck and skull were not designed for this.

(2) Now rotate each shoulder separately using tiny movements, but concentrating on just the shoulder sockets, not the arms. Try five rotations forwards and five backwards, first with the right shoulder, then the left.

(3) Your neck and shoulder muscles should now be less tense. Ensure that your head feels well-balanced, not jutting forward as this puts tension on the neck. Check to see that your shoulders are relaxed, not creeping back up to the ears with tension! Is the back of the chair still supporting the base of your spine?

(4) Now relax each muscle group, working up through the body, starting with the feet and ankles.

(5) Give your toes a little wriggle to identify the muscles in your feet. Now concentrate just on your feet and ankles, feeling them grow heavy as they sink into the floor.

(6) Now consciously release the tension from your calf muscles and knees. Feel your legs falling outwards as your knees and calves relax.

(7) Your thighs should be feeling heavy as they press into the seat of the chair. Let their weight sink into the chair. Relax the muscles of the thighs and hips.

(8) Think about your tummy as it rises and falls gently with your breathing. Don't hold it in. Be conscious of it expanding with each breath.

(9) Relax your chest as you continue to breathe in and out. Be conscious of the rise and fall; gentle inhalation and exhalation of air.

(10) Let your arms get heavy, feel the pressure of your hands in your lap. Relax your wrists. Be conscious of any tension left in your hands and let them lie loosely in your lap.

(11) Is your head still well balanced on your shoulders? Concentrate on this balance to the head and neck.

(12) Close your eyes. Take a deep breath in through your nose ... and let it out slowly, through your mouth. Take another deep breath ... and let it out slowly. With each breath, feel your body getting more heavy and sinking into the chair.

(13) Slowly, in your own time, open your eyes. Gently wriggle fingers and toes. If you want, shake out arm and leg muscles. Have a little stretch, before standing up, hopefully refreshed and less tense.

Step 4: Take comments and field any questions Thank the group for participating. Ask for comments. Explain that there are many different relaxation techniques; this may not have suited some people, but it does have the advantage of being as short or long a session as individuals need, can be practised almost anywhere at any time, and drawn upon when energy is flagging, or when individuals feel the need to control tension.

Step 5: Sum up by referring to the objectives

RELAXATION 2

A more active type of tension control exercise than **Relaxation 1**, this involves stretching and bending, but no lying on the floor. All relaxation exercises are invaluable for those who become tense and nervous – before a difficult meeting, for example – or who need to unwind after coping with a stressful situation.

For this activity, loose fitting, suitable clothing is preferable, but not essential.

Objectives By the end of this activity participants will:

- have learnt and practised a technique for tension control;
- be able to assess whether this method might be appropriate for their own needs.

Resources None.

Time 5–10 minutes.

Method

Step 1: Explain the technique You will need floor-space, and somewhere quiet to do this exercise. Unlike relaxation techniques that can be done sitting at home, at your desk, or in your car seat, this activity requires stretching and bending – not to be practised at the supermarket, or in a bus queue, unless in exceptional circumstances!

Step 2: Set up the activity Each participant should find sufficient floor-space to exercise. The military system of holding arms out to the side so that you are no closer than fingertip touching space from your neighbour can be employed if floor-space is limited.

Step 3: Talk participants through the relaxation technique

(1) Stand tall, feet hip-width apart, weight evenly balanced.

(2) Stretch up arms to the ceiling, splaying the fingers, standing as high as you can on tiptoe. Push and stretch to reach as high as you can. Really push for the sky!

(3) Gradually relax the tension, lowering heels to the floor and letting hands and wrists drop, while still keeping arms in the air. Let your hands really flop at the wrists.

(4) Next, lowering your upper arms horizontally out from the body, let your lower arms flop, so that the backs of your hands rest at the sides of your face.

(5) Now let your arms drop loosely at your sides. Don't slump, but let your shoulders fall. Feel the weight of those relaxed arms.

(6) Let your upper body flop from the waist. Feel as if you are hanging over a washing line, torso relaxed, arms hanging heavy and loose. Let your head just fall. Don't put any pressure on the neck.

(7) Bend knees slightly so that your legs still support you, but are relaxed. Breathe gently and easily.

(8) Bounce very gently, feeling your spine being stretched out.

(9) Concentrate on your spine as very slowly, vertebra by vertebra, you uncurl and return to the upright position.

Step 4: Sum up, and close the activity referring to the objectives No single technique will suit everyone. Relaxation is a skill and like all skills needs to be practised. If you are habitually tense, or unused to physical exercise of this sort, you may find this technique difficult, even uncomfortable at first. However, with perseverance, it will become easier – and you will know that you have achieved muscle relaxation when you can flop at will with no discomfort!

Relaxation 3

This is another technique which can be performed anywhere, at any time, when the need to calm down is felt. It is based on Pranayama Yoga breathing exercises and involves a combination of breath and abdominal muscle control. It is probably best *not* to practise this on a full stomach!

Objectives By the end of this activity participants will:

- have learnt and practised a technique for tension control;
- be able to assess whether this method might be appropriate for their own needs.

Resources Copy of the handout for each person.

Time 10–15 minutes.

Method
Step 1: Explain the technique This technique is based on a principle of Pranayama Yoga. Prana means breath control and Yama means relaxation of the mind. By using a simple combination of breathing patterns and abdominal control, non-assertive feelings, whether tending towards the passive (nervousness, anxiety, self-consciousness) or aggressive (anger, tension, frustration) can be calmed.

This is just to give participants a taste of the technique. It needs to be practised, quietly at home, and each stage perfected before moving to the next.

Step 2: Set up the activity Participants should sit comfortably – but not slumped – either in an upright chair or on the floor if preferred.

Step 3: Talk participants through the relaxation technique

(1) Breathing normally, concentrate on the tummy. Pull it in as far as you can; try to flatten it against the backbone! Now flop it out again letting it relax. Do this a couple more times.

(2) Now try this pulling in and flopping out pattern to a rhythm. *In* – one, two; *Out* – one, two. Concentrate on dividing each movement into halves – tummy in half the way, then all the way; tummy out half the way, then all the way.

(3) In your own time, gradually increase the count – in for three, out for three (divide each movement into thirds); in for four, out for four (divide each movement into quarters). You should divide these movements up into tinier subdivisions – in and out – but should keep the action as smooth as possible. To be effective, you should aim to be able to hold for a count of six in and six out (although skilled practitioners of Pranayama Yoga progress to a count of 15).

(4) Stop the stomach control exercises, while concentrating on breathing. Keeping a straight back, take slow, deep breaths in and out through the nose. The slower the breathing, the more calming it will be.

(5) Now try to combine the tummy and breathing exercises. Pull the tummy in for the count of one, hold in while breathing in and out slowly through the nose, then relax the tummy for one. Repeat this until it becomes a natural rhythm.

(6) Begin increasing the count – tummy in for two; hold while breathing slowly in and out; tummy out for the count of two, and so on. Do not try to get up to the count of six now. Practise at home as this technique will take some weeks to perfect.

(7) When you feel comfortable with this rhythm there are variations designed to produce relaxation, peace of mind and energy. Try this: breathe in slowly and deeply through the nose and hold the breath. Tummy in for the count of one; breathe out slowly through the nose; tummy out for the count of one. Keep this pattern going, gradually increasing the tummy hold count.

Step 4: Take any comments from the group. Issue the Handout As it is unlikely that you will be an expert in Pranayama Yoga, participants who would like to take this further should be referred to their local Adult Education department for courses in your area.

The Handout suggests two variations on the Pranayama theme –

the first to control moments of panic, and the second to control anger or temper – both extremes of the assertiveness spectrum which hopefully you will never need to put into practice!

Step 5: Close the activity referring back to the objectives

HANDOUT

Relaxation 3

Breath control exercises

These exercises are based on the Pranayama Yoga technique to relax the mind and body. Prana means breath control and Yama means relaxation of the mind.

Sitting comfortably, with a straight back, pull in the tummy towards the backbone, then flop it out and relax. Repeat this a few times, breathing normally.

Now add the rhythm – tummy in for the count of one; out for the count of one. Repeat a few times, then increase the count – tummy in for the count of two; out for the count of two. Remember to concentrate on subdividing each movement: *In* – one, two, three; *Out* – one, two, three. Continue increasing the count until you can comfortably hold the tummy in for the count of six, then relax it out to the count of six.

Leave the tummy control for a few minutes and concentrate on breathing. Make sure you are still sitting upright with a straight back. Take slow, deep breaths in and out through the nose. Remember, the slower the breathing, the greater will be the tension control.

Now combine the tummy and breath control. Pull tummy in for the count of one; hold it. Breathe in and out slowly through the nose. Relax the tummy to the count of one. Repeat until rhythm is established, then increase the tummy control to the count of two – take tummy in using two small abdominal pulls; hold it. Breathe in and out slowly and gently. Relax the tummy out – one, two. Continue to practise this until a count of six can be achieved, breathing in and out just once between each abdominal tightening and relaxing.

An alternative pattern can be practised. Breathe in through the nose and hold the breath. Pull in the tummy to the count of one. Hold it while letting out the breath, slowly, through the nose. Relax the tummy to the count of one. Again, repeat until comfortable with the rhythm, then begin increasing the tummy control counts until you can hold to the count of six.

Panic control

Pull in the tummy, tightly towards the backbone, for the count of one. Hold your breath for 5 seconds. Now breathe in and out slowly through the nose, still holding the tummy in. Relax the tummy, pushing it out, to the count of one. Concentrate on abdominal control and breathing rhythms. Increase the tummy control to the count of two, then three, four, five and six, still keeping the same breathing patterns.

When feeling anxious and panicky, there is a tendency to hyper-ventilate – to breathe too quickly and shallowly. Our hearts thud, and it is difficult to breathe deeply because our tummy muscles feel tense and knotted. This, in itself, increases the feeling of agitation. By concentrating on deep breathing *and abdominal control*, this technique (which can be practised, undetected by others) quickly calms and relaxes.

Anger/temper control

Pull in the tummy, tightly towards the backbone, for the count of one. Hold the breath for 5 seconds. Push the tummy out to the count of one. Breathe in and out. Pull the tummy in for two equal controls. Hold the breath for 10 seconds, then relax the tummy using two equal controls. Breathe in and out. Concentrate on the counting and the pattern you are creating. Take the tummy in for three equal counts. Hold the breath for 15 seconds. Relax the tummy for three. Do not increase the counts any further.

Repeat this exercise twice a day, night and morning, and you should feel less tense.

RELAXATION 4

When behaving in a non-assertive way, we often take ourselves (and others) too seriously. We may feel ineffective or inadequate or might see insult or censure where none was intended. This causes tension in the body and a feeling of unease. Laughter is the furthest thing from our minds, and yet it has been proven that laughter can, indeed, be the best medicine for releasing tension. This activity uses laughter as a means of relaxation.

Objectives By the end of this activity participants will:

- have learnt and practised a technique for releasing tension.

Resources (*Optional*) – Notepaper, pencils/pens, flipchart and marker.

Time 5–15 minutes.

Method

Step 1: Set up the activity It is best to set up this activity without too much preamble. Just clear enough space in the centre of the room for the group to stand in a circle, holding hands, facing inwards.

Step 2: Explain the activity Without letting go of hands, the whole group must now devise a way of turning the circle so that everyone faces outwards.

Step 3: Begin the activity Let the contortions continue until either the task has been achieved, or every one is laughing at the attempt.

Step 4: Halt the activity Allow participants a few moments to settle down and return to their chairs.

Step 5: Process the activity Explain that the object of the exercise was not the task itself, but achieving laughter by some means. Other methods could have been adopted. However, one important aspect of this activity was the physical contact by holding hands. Laughter is infectious, and the energy created can pass around the circle through contact.

Laughter is one of the best ways to relieve tension; we should learn to laugh at ourselves and *with* others at every opportunity. Laughter therapy has proved very beneficial in alleviating stress of all kinds.

(*Optional Steps*)
Step 6: Suggestions for follow-up work Unlike some other relaxation techniques, it is unlikely that participants would want to repeat this particular experience on a regular basis! However, the ability to laugh should be nurtured.

Ask participants to spend a few minutes jotting down things which make them laugh.

Step 7: Lead a short discussion on things which make people laugh You could write up a list on the flipchart. By exchanging ideas, the suggestions of others may be helpful to those who find it hard to think of anything which makes them laugh.

Step 8: Close the activity Encourage participants to add to their lists if possible, and to avail themselves of laughter aids – videos which they find amusing; books or magazines, and so on. Recognize friends who share their sense of humour so that they can enjoy laughter in their company.

RELAXATION 5

This relaxation method was devised by Dorothy Sarnoff, an American communication expert. She calls it the 'Sarnoff Squeeze'. It is an unobtrusive and effective way to control nervousness and reduce negative feelings such as anger and stress.

Objectives By the end of this activity participants will:

- have learnt and practised a technique for tension control;
- be able to assess whether this method might be appropriate for their own needs.

Resources None.

Time 5 minutes.

Method

Step 1: Explain the activity This exercise is based on the principle of tightening then relaxing muscles while breathing deeply and slowly. It concentrates on just one set of muscles – the abdominal triangle below the ribs where they begin to splay. This method was perfected by Dorothy Sarnoff, an American speech expert, and is known as the 'Sarnoff Squeeze'.* It is another exercise that, once perfected, can be used at any time without others being aware that you are using a technique to prevent nervousness, relieve anxiety, or defuse anger. Because it involves tensing then relaxing the muscles under the

* Dorothy Sarnoff: *Never be Nervous Again* (1988). Century Hutchinson Ltd, London.

diaphragm, it has the added advantage of aiding voice control – you will be able to talk without a nervous tremble, and project without raising your voice or shouting.

Step 2: Set up the activity Participants should sit comfortably in their chairs, with a straight back, but inclined slightly forward.

Step 3: Talk participants through the relaxation technique

(1) To identify the muscle group, put the palms of your hands together, fingers pointing upwards, elbows raised so that your forearms are horizontal to the floor.
(2) Push your hands together until you feel the force in the heels of the palms and under your arms.
(3) Breathe in, then let out the breath, slowly and gently, through a slightly open mouth, and using a soft hiss – sounding like 'ssssss…'. While breathing out, tighten the muscles in that triangle between the ribs. Relax the muscles at the end of the exhalation. Breathe in gently.

Dorothy Sarnoff provides a useful image to remember, so that you can practise the 'Squeeze', anywhere, without anyone knowing. Identify the triangle of muscle by imagining that you are rowing a boat against a strong current, pulling the oars back and up. This will contract the right set of muscles. Remember to contract these muscles as you are breathing *Out*, slowly, with a quiet hiss. Relax the triangle of muscle at the end of the exhalation. Breathe in again gently.

Step 4: Close the activity, referring to the objectives

RELAXATION 6

Like **Relaxation 4** this activity might generate some laughter, although that is not the object of the exercise. However, 'laughter is the best medicine' it is said, so perhaps this is not a bad thing! This activity helps relaxation, but also relates to posture, image and body language.

Objectives By the end of this activity participants will:

- have learnt and practised a technique for tension control;
- be able to assess whether this method might be appropriate for their own needs.

Resources None.

Time 5 minutes.

Method
Step 1: Explain the technique This exercise is designed to relieve the tension in the neck and shoulders. If morale is low; if we have poor self-esteem or are feeling particularly ineffective or insecure, our body language mirrors this. Posture suffers. Image suffers. Shoulders slump, and our heads droop. As our heads weigh between 10 and 14 pounds, this slouching puts undue pressure on the neck with resulting tight muscles, and possible neck pain and headaches. If we are feeling irritated, angry or stressed we tend to 'lead with our chins', thrusting our heads forward. This, too, creates tension in the neck and shoulders. Practise this exercise if you feel particularly tense or anxious.

Step 2: Set up the activity Clear enough space for participants to walk around the room.

Step 3: Talk participants through the relaxation technique

(1) Stand tall, feet slightly apart, heels on the floor, but with the weight on the balls of the feet. Feel as if an invisible string is attached to the top of your head, gently pulling you vertical. Let arms and hands hang loosely at your sides.
(2) Let your head fall forward towards your chest, then gently and smoothly return head to upright position. Let it fall back – gently – to gradually stretch out the muscles of the neck. Repeat this nodding action – slowly and smoothly – until it becomes a natural rhythm.
(3) Begin to walk around the room, still nodding your head gently down to the chest and back; down and back.

N.B. This is where participants may get a fit of the giggles as each simulates a nodding dog in the back of a 1960s car! If the group does begin to laugh, that's fine. Allow a few moments for laughter before recommencing. This exercise is easier to do alone, perhaps!

(4) Stand tall again. If there is still some stiffness in the neck, a little massage of the tendons at the back of the neck and a gentle shrug and circling of the shoulders should help release remaining tension.

Step 4: Close the activity by referring to the objectives

CHAPTER 8

CLOSURES

GIFTS

This activity is about giving and receiving compliments. Unless participants knew each other well prior to attending, it should be run at the end of a course of more than one day's duration.

Objectives By the end of this activity participants will:

- have given a compliment to every participant on the course;
- have received a compliment from every participant on the course;
- have analysed the feelings connected with both.

Resources Sheet of A4 paper for each participant, notepaper, pens, tables, or facility for lap-top writing.

Time 30–45 minutes.

Method
Step 1: Introduce the activity Compliments are like gifts, but often cause embarrassment to the giver, receiver, or both. Often we do not give compliments for fear that our intentions may be misinterpreted, or that the compliment will be rejected – thrown back at us. We are poor at receiving compliments, often because of a misguided view of modesty; sometimes because we feel uneasy or threatened by them.

When self-esteem and confidence are low it is difficult to appreciate other people's positive views of us. We are either not sure whether to believe the compliment, or feel that we are *not*, in fact, good at ... or that we haven't the personality, skills or whatever suggested by the other person. Because both giving and receiving compliments can be risky if not handled assertively by both parties, they are often neglected elements in our repertoire of communication skills.

This activity gives participants the opportunity to give and receive compliments without having to make an immediate, spontaneous response. However, at the end of the activity they will have the opportunity to acknowledge the 'gifts' in whichever way they choose.

Step 2: Explain procedure and timings Each participant will receive a sheet of paper (and pen if required). They will write their own name in bold letters at the top of the sheet, then place the paper on the floor in the middle of the room. Each participant will collect one paper at a time, and on it write a compliment to the named person. Having done so, they return that paper to the centre of the room, and collect another. This continues until every participant has written a compliment to every other course member, ie annotated every sheet.

Individuals may decide whether or not they want to sign their name to compliments, but by this random choice method of selection, rather than just handing the sheets in a clockwise or anti-clockwise direction around the group, anonymity can be maintained if desired.

A time for reflection will be given initially – 2 or 3 minutes – when participants should consider what compliment they would like to pay each person. Compliments can be about personality, looks, clothes, skills and so on, and must be genuine. If participants know each other outside the course, they may wish to use prior knowledge for the compliment. However, in order to keep within any confidentiality agreement, the compliment should not name names, eg 'I liked the way you treated two people fairly last week' not 'I liked the way you sorted out that row between Ben and Maria'. Compliments should be specific, eg 'You've beautiful hair' could be written as 'You've beautiful hair; your choice of style suits the shape of your face' or 'I like your smile' could be 'Your whole face lights up when you smile'.

Participants should try to think of different compliments to pay each colleague (so that no sheet is just a series of duplications, eg 'I admire your honesty' written a dozen times) but if individuals feel

strongly about a trait already mentioned on a person's sheet, this is reinforcing a positive image and therefore perfectly valid.

Approximately two minutes will be given for the writing of each 'gift'.

Step 3: Begin activity Issue a sheet of paper to each participant. Instruct them to write their names on the top and place the sheet in the middle of the room; then to spend a few moments thinking about their colleagues and how they are going to phrase each compliment. Rough notepaper should be available for those who want to jot down ideas before filling in individuals' sheets.

Step 4: After a few minutes reflection time, instruct participants to collect a sheet (obviously not their own!) from the middle of the room, to consider and then write a compliment to the person named at the top of the sheet They should find a table or quiet space in the room to work.

Step 5: After two minutes, check that everyone has finished writing a compliment to the named person. Instruct them to return that sheet to the middle of room, and to collect another, different sheet It may be that after a short while, when participants become used to the activity, two minutes becomes too long before change-over. However, the group must exercise patience and work at the pace of the slowest without that person feeling pressurised to speed up!

Step 6: Continue as in Step 5 until each person has written a compliment to every other course member By the end of this exercise, the change-over can become quite chaotic with participants searching for named sheets they have not yet worked on. This 'fun' aspect should be encouraged; it keeps the activity light, and feelings positive.

Step 7: Participants should collect their own paper from the centre of the room Allow time for individuals to read and digest the 'gifts' from their colleagues.

Step 8: Allow time for participants to respond by thanking individuals (or the group) for the 'gift' Participants should be encouraged to respond assertively to the compliments. For example, if someone has signed their name to a compliment 'I admire your clothes sense – how your scarves, shoes, jewellery are colour co-ordinated', an appropriate response to that person might be a simple 'Thank you, Chris' or something like 'Thank you; I try to buy accessories which tone with

my clothes', rather than 'It's just a fluke – I fling a few bits and pieces together and hope it looks OK' or 'It's someone else's taste, not mine – I bought it all from a second-hand stall'.

Step 9: Process the activity Begin by getting general reactions to the exercise itself – did people find it enjoyable, difficult, easier or harder than giving compliments face to face and so on.

Questions you might use:

- How did you feel about giving compliments?
- Which was easier, giving or receiving? Why?
- Which is *usually* more difficult for you, giving or receiving compliments? Why?
- Why do people sometimes feel uncomfortable about giving compliments. Is it the same in any context?
- Why do we sometimes feel uncomfortable receiving compliments?
- Were you surprised by any of the compliments you received today? Why?
- Were you pleased with any particular compliment you received? Why?
- What have you learnt about giving and receiving compliments?

Step 10: Close the activity, referring to the objectives Each person has, to take away with them, a collection of compliments from course colleagues and the recommendation that they value all the positive 'gifts' they have received. They should refer to these sheets to remind themselves of qualities other people have recognized in them, and appreciated.

KEEP UP THE GOOD WORK

This is a post-course activity which combines networking with a vehicle for continuing practice of assertion skills.

Objectives By the end of this activity participants will:

- have identified course colleagues with whom they will keep in touch;
- have made a commitment to continue to practise assertion skills at home, in their social life and/or at their place of work;
- have made a commitment to contact and give advice and feedback to course colleagues.

N.B. This activity relies on the goodwill of participants, their willingness to continue to practise assertiveness after the course, and to network with course colleagues. This needs to be established at the outset.

Resources A copy of the two-leaved Exercise Sheet for each participant, pen/pencils, (*optional*) – Copy of each participant's personal training programme – see **Ladder of success**.

Time 30–45 minutes of training course time. Participants must also be prepared to offer telephone time to colleagues during the weeks after the course, or agree to meet to discuss progress.

Method

Step 1: Introduce the activity It is far easier to be motivated and to practise skills in the environment of a training programme, with the support and advice of like-minded people. It is sometimes difficult to

maintain progress after the course has finished – all too easy to fall back into old ways of working, or ineffective behaviour patterns. This activity is designed to help participants maintain their learning and practice through continued support from course colleagues.

Step 2: Explain what is required by referring to the objectives. Gain commitment from participants (see Note above) Participants will be required to choose a situation where they would like to be more assertive, and which has not yet been tackled. If they have a personal training record as suggested by the activity **Ladder of success**, this will probably be the next item prioritised. They will have some time now to talk over with colleagues their proposed approach to their problem. They will then exchange telephone numbers and agree to contact each other after a specified time to check on progress, and offer support and advice.

If anyone is not prepared to give a contact number or doesn't want to participate in this post-course follow-up, then their wishes should be honoured. They can still participate in Steps 3 to 5.

Step 3: Allow a few minutes for participants to identify a problem area on which they intend to work after the course This can be work, social or home based.

Step 4: Divide the group into pairs or smaller groups of 3 or 4 people These groupings should be of people who have worked well together during the training; who respect each other's opinions and who will offer constructive post-course support. Participants may wish to choose their own groupings.

Step 5: Instruct groups to talk over each other's problems, to clearly define the situation to be tackled, and to offer advice on how to progress The groups will need to consider things such as:

- How specific is the aim?
- Is there more than one issue, within the situation, which needs to be tackled?
- Can these issues be prioritized?
- What are the risks involved?
- How is it best to proceed?
- What obstacles to success can be seen?
- How might these obstacles be pre-empted and overcome?
- When and where is the best time and place to tackle this situation?

If there is time, groups could help individuals rehearse their opening lines (see the activity on initiating difficult conversations, **Be prepared**).

Step 6: Issue the two-leaved Exercise Sheet to everyone who has agreed to network Instruct participants to duplicate the information required on the sheet so that each member of their small group has a copy for their retention. The original stays with the owner.

Step 7: Instruct participants to arrange a convenient time for follow-up contact This should not be too long after the course.

Step 8: Check that there are no difficulties, and that everyone who wishes to network has exchanged telephone numbers It may well be that other participants, not within the small working groups of this activity, would like to keep in touch for mutual support. This should be encouraged as often individuals can feel very alone without the support of the group.

Step 9: Close the activity

EXERCISE SHEET

Keep up the good work

Duplicate the information required (using the additional sheet(s) if necessary) so that each member of your group has a copy. *Don't forget a copy for yourself.*

NAME ______________________________

TELEPHONE NUMBER ______________________________

SITUATION ______________________________

____

____

____

DATE FOR CONTACT ______________________________

✂- -

NAME ______________________________

TELEPHONE NUMBER ______________________________

SITUATION ______________________________

____

____

____

DATE FOR CONTACT ______________________________

____

NAME ______________________________

TELEPHONE NUMBER ______________________________

SITUATION ______________________________

DATE FOR CONTACT ______________________________

NAME ______________________________

TELEPHONE NUMBER ______________________________

SITUATION ______________________________

DATE FOR CONTACT ______________________________

CHECK IT OUT

A post-course activity, **Check it out** gives participants a checklist for planning potentially difficult encounters where assertiveness skills are called for.

Objectives By the end of this activity participants will:

- have a format to follow for planning a difficult encounter.

Resources One copy of the Handout for each participant.

Time To be completed in participants' own time, as and when required, for post-course assertive action.

Method:
Step 1: Explain the activity With continued practice, assertive behaviour will become a choice which is second nature. However, there will be times when a particularly difficult situation looms; the chances of reaching a mutually satisfactory resolution will be enhanced by forward planning and rehearsal of assertive behaviour.

Participants will be issued with a Handout which can be used as a checklist whenever a potentially difficult situation or interpersonal conflict is to be tackled.

Step 2: Issue the Handout. Field any questions The Handout is not for immediate use, but as a reference for participants to use after the course.

Step 3: Sum up, then close the activity The list on the Handout may look a bit daunting at first sight, but remember that, through training,

you have the ability to tackle any situation in an assertive way, however the other person reacts. Assertiveness is about choice. You have the right to assert yourself – but you also have the right to choose alternative behaviour if appropriate and 'right' for that particular occasion.

HANDOUT

Check it out

Consider the following points before embarking on a difficult encounter.

(1) What, exactly, do I want to achieve from this interaction?
(2) In terms of behaviour choices, what are my options?
(3) What do I usually do in this kind of situation?
(4) How will assertive behaviour help me accomplish my goal?
(5) What are the advantages of adopting assertive behaviour?
(6) What are the risks involved? What might stop me from asserting myself?
(7) What are my rights in this situation? What are the other person's rights?
(8) Am I well prepared for this encounter? Do I have relevant facts at my fingertips? Am I relaxed and mentally prepared?
(9) How will I let the other person know that I have listened, heard and understood?
(10) How will I let the other person know how I feel?
(11) What are my opening words/lines going to be?
(12) What techniques do I have for dealing with their dismissiveness, anger, defensiveness, sarcasm, stubbornness, etc?